PARTICIPATIVE MANAGEMENT: EMPLOYEE-MANAGEMENT COOPERATION
A Practical Approach

Books by Joseph P. Cangemi

Higher Education and the Development of Self-Actualizing Personalities (1977).

Effective Leadership—A Humanistic Perspective (1980). Coauthored with George Guttschalk.

Higher Education In the United States and Latin America (1982). Coauthored with Casimir Kowalski.

La Gerencia Participativa (1983). Published by La Sociedad Colombiana De Inginieros Industriales Y Administradores, Colombia, South America.

Perspectives in Higher Education (1983). Coauthored with Casimir Kowalski.

Participative Management: Employee-Management Cooperation—A Practical Approach (1985). Coauthored with Casimir Kowalski and Jeffrey Claypool.

Books by Casimir J. Kowalski

The Impact of College on Persisting and Nonpersisting Students (1976).

Higher Education in the United States and Latin America (1982). Coauthored with Joseph Cangemi.

Perspectives in Higher Education (1983). Coauthored with Joseph Cangemi.

Participative Management: Employee-Management Cooperation—A Practical Approach (1985). Coauthored with Joseph Cangemi and Jeffrey Claypool.

PARTICIPATIVE MANAGEMENT: EMPLOYEE-MANAGEMENT COOPERATION
A Practical Approach

Joseph P. Cangemi
Casimir J. Kowalski
Jeffrey C. Claypool

Philosophical Library
New York

Library of Congress Cataloging in Publication Data
Main Entry under title:

Participative management.

1. Management—United States—Employee participation
—Addresses, essays, lectures.   I. Cangemi, Joseph P.
II. Kowalski, Casimir.   III. Claypool, Jeffrey C.
HD5660.U5p37   1984   658.3'152   84-16627
ISBN 0-8022-2422-9

ISBN 8022-2422-9
Copyright 1985 by Philosophical Library, Inc.
200 West 57 Street, New York, N.Y. 10019.
Manufactured in the United States of America.

This book is dedicated to
those leaders who believe that an
organization's future is secured
through the continued development
of its employees.

Once a century a man may be ruined or made insufferable by praise. But surely once a minute something generous dies for want of it.

—John Masefield

Foreword

This book by a group of noted scholars is, to my mind, a valuable aid to the modern manager. The economic turmoil of recent times has forced the business community in the United States to re-examine its traditional view of the work place. Clearly, America's business community recognizes the pressing need to improve productivity. While America has experienced improvements in productivity with greater use of automation, it is through improvements in worker motivation that truly significant productivity gains can be achieved in the future.

All of the scholars in this book focus on the role of business management and corporate philosophy toward the work place and how a humanistic approach to employees can help affect productivity. The humanistic approach is now a critical element in an effective management and these scholars show how to implement this policy.

Cary W. Blankenship
Commissioner
Kentucky Department of
Economic Development

vii

Preface

American business people long have believed that the mainstays of business are finance, manufacturing, marketing, and—since World War II—research and development. If an organization performs well in these areas, it supposedly meets all the requirements of a successful business. Subservient to the foregoing because of its customary secondary status has been human resource management. But during the last twenty years, something has gone awry. Obsolete technologies, energy crunches, crumbling ivory towers, Japanese business concepts—all have induced business to search for a better way of managing. This book provides possible clues for those searching in the human resource management area.

The authors of this book provide insight into what many managers now feel may be an equally important function of business: to manage human resources in a way that the total work force performs up to its potential—physically, mentally, and emotionally.

The book proposes a variety of approaches to an understanding of participative management that has practical value for the student not long out of school, as well as for those who have worked in the business world a number of years.

Recent graduates, reflecting on their entry into the business world, often admit to a lonely confusion they felt at the time. How many hours and years did they waste, waiting for recognition and responsibility? And, not receiving these, how many packed their bags for more fertile fields?

The personal difficulties encountered by many warrant a search by social scientists and experienced practitioners for better ways of understanding the ingredients in successfully managed organizations—and of possible trends in the future.

How to determine and recognize the right employer, the right boss, are procedures described in this book for those individuals looking for something more than just a nine-to-five existence.

For those now engrossed in managing business organizations who want improvement and constructive change, this book provides participative management concepts from a cross section of senior business professionals and academic practitioners. All describe what occurs when the human side of an organization is promoted within the framework of an American enterprise.

Most leaders in organizations are too involved with day-to-day struggles and concerns about the bottom line to analyze how organizations ought to be structured. The management techniques described herein may indicate a whole new direction for those not accustomed to utilizing the total brainpower in an organization. The writers subscribe to the notion that when everyone understands and is committed to the mission of an organization, there will be a dedicated effort to achieve organizational goals. Furthermore, participative managing is not "natural"; that is, it is a learned style and does not come about easily. Once achieved, the rewards exceed all expectations so much that companies sometimes shy away from publicity on the subject (Robert Townsend, *Further Up the Organization*, 1979).

We appreciate the time and effort the authors have expended in sharing their knowledge and beliefs about a successful way of managing organized groups of people. Our special thanks go to the authors, who contributed and blended their thoughts for students on the art of managing—who are always reaching for a better way.

William R. Miller
Vice President, Director of
Human Resources
Century Electronics, Inc.
St. Louis, Missouri

Formerly
Vice President, Human Resources
Gould Corporation

Contents

Related Articles

Contributing Authors

DR. J. RICHARD BRYSON is President, Marion Technical College, Marion, Ohio.

DR. JOSPEH P. CANGEMI is Professor of Psychology, Western Kentucky University, and a consultant to numerous *Fortune 500* corporations.

DR. RICHARD CARD is Superintendent of Schools, Fryeburg, Maine.

JEFFREY C. CLAYPOOL has been a career employee of Firestone Tire and Rubber Company. His present position is Manager, Personnel and Management Development, Firestone Tire and Rubber Company, Akron, Ohio.

DR. DONALD W. COLE, President, Organization Development Institute, Chesterland, Ohio, is widely regarded for his contributions to the field of organization development.

DR. JAMES R. CRAIG is Professor of Psychology, Western Kentucky University, Bowling Green, Kentucky.

GORDON E. DEMARCO is past Corporate Manager, Waste Control, Firestone Tire and Rubber Company, Akron, Ohio.

DR. CHARLES L. EISON, Administrator in the Office of Grants and Contracts, Western Kentucky University, Bowling Green, Kentucky, is also Associate Professor of Psychology at the same institution.

KATHRYN L. HERKELMANN, employed by General Motors Corporation, Corvette Assembly Plant, Bowling Green, Kentucky, is Supervisor, Salaried Personnel Administration.

xiii

Tom W. Hollopeter is President, Innovative Management Systems, Inc., Oklahoma City, Oklahoma.

Dr. Casimir J. Kowalski is President, Alliance College, Cambridge Springs, Pennsylvania.

Dr. Richard L. Miller, a licensed psychologist, is Professor of Psychology, Western Kentucky University and a consultant in employee/management relations.

William R. Miller is Vice-President of Human Resource Development, Century Electronics, St. Louis, Missouri.

Dr. Josip Obradovic is Dean of the School of Social Work of the University of Zagreb, Zagreb, Yugoslavia.

Richard Alan Potter is Vice President, American National Bank and Trust Company, Bowling Green, Kentucky.

Dr. Charles M. Ray is Professor of Administrative Office Systems, College of Business Administration, Western Kentucky University, Bowling Green, Kentucky.

James E. Stirrett is Personnel Manager, Firestone Tire and Rubber Company, Decatur, Illinois.

Dr. Raymond G. Taylor, Jr. is Superintendent of Schools, Augusta, Maine.

William L. Taylor is a career officer in the United States Army.

Ted R. Tompkins, past Manager, Labor Relations, Firestone Canada, presently serves as Plant Manager, Firestone Tire and Rubber Company, Hamilton, Canada.

Gar Trusley is President, Gar Trusley and Associates, of Westerville, Ohio.

Dr. Luis A. Zarruk, is Vice President of Finance of Hilanderias del Fonce, Bucaramanga, Columbia.

Authors' Preface

The authors of this book are encouraged by the increasing numbers of organizations that support the concept of participative management. Indeed, participative management has become the buzzword in management circles for the 80s.

There is mounting evidence that a participatory style of leadership behavior is highly related to improved and more effective work performance—and hence increased profits. Improving worker effectiveness and increasing an organization's profits are not only sensible and good business, they are a mandate for survival in the 80s and 90s.

The three authors have substantial combined experience in participative management concepts. They decided that a book focusing on different aspects of participatory management behavior could make a contribution to many managers in the field, especially those who raise numerous questions about the concept of participative management and its organizational implementations.

In this regard, the authors sought contributions from practitioners in the field, as well as input from academic-oriented colleagues. The result, the authors believe, is a reasonably balanced text of the theory, issues, art and practice of participatory management. Added to these articles are several related articles which the authors felt rounded out the text even further.

Many of the authors of articles appearing in this book wrote the articles especially for this book. The authors wish to thank them for their contribution. The authors also wish to thank Rose Morse of Philosophical Library for her never tiring assistance and patience. Without her efforts this book could never have become a reality.

Joseph Cangemi
Casimir Kowalski
Jeffrey Claypool

October 1, 1984

A Pragmatist's View of Participative Management

Joseph P. Cangemi

Dealing with people and organizations is my chosen vocation, especially business and industrial enterprises—both union and nonunion. To date, I have had the opportunity to work with over 20,000 individuals in both small and large groups, as well as individually, in the United States and in several foreign countries as well. I have served and counseled both presidents and floor sweepers, and all the layers of employees in between. These types of experiences and relationships have given me the perspective to judge, at least in my own thinking, just what it is that seems to turn people on so they will want to give improved performance and contribute significantly to their organizations, rather than render mediocre activity or do merely what is expected of them so they can keep their jobs. There is little question, in my view—based on twenty years of experience and observations—there *is* a form of leadership behavior which will yield consistent, superior results in terms of better-than-average employee

This paper was prepared for presentation at the International Plant Managers' Conference, Firestone Tire and Rubber Company, Oklahoma City, Oklahoma, November 11 and 12, 1982.

performance, employee cooperation, and employee attitudes. This style of leadership behavior is employee-oriented; it is referred to today as *Participative Management*. Indeed, the professional literature likewise supports participative management for its positive impact on organizations (Flory, 1965; Miles, 1975; Frost, 1974; Ouchi, 1981; Meltzer, 1976; Cangemi, 1980; Gellerman, 1963; Maslow, 1974; Ritchie, 1976; Sutermeister, 1976; Scanlan and Atherton, 1981).

Two major concerns of management today are employee attitude and productivity. Management has always been concerned with these two behaviors. The only difference today, however, is that management is more seriously open to considering participative approaches to the problem, whereas such approaches were but fleeting discussions just a few years ago. Today more managers seem interested in *understanding* their employees and *their needs* than at any time since the Industrial Revolution. And with good reason: such concern usually leads to improved profit generation (Likert, 1967). In other words, it is good business.

Participative Management and Employees' Needs

From the time an individual is conceived until he dies, there appears to be a tendency in the organism to grow, to unfold, to become more and more of what he is capable of becoming, to fulfill the potential locked in the genes (Erickson, 1963). My own observations are that people who do not grow in some way become bottled up and / or twisted inside. They seem to be aimless, goal-deficient, have a dislike both for themselves and authority, have poor interpersonal relationships, or become so inward they find it difficult to communicate with anyone, including their families. In short, it is obvious that whatever talent and potential they have, they do not use it, or feel they cannot use it, and this blocking of the growth process appears to create many of the behaviors cited above (Maslow, 1974). After working with numerous individuals plagued by this behavior, and observing how impotent and negative they feel about themselves, the words of one behavioral scientist seem to make some sense: GROW OR DIE! It is apparent we must become concerned with more than physical death; we also must become concerned with the *mental* death of human beings.

In working with numerous factories and businesses and studying management-employee relationships within them, I began to notice some consistent behavior patterns of employees. Employees who did nothing but work on machines all day and who rarely did anything else but routine work seemed to *lose* something of themselves. If they worked in an environment where it was difficult *to see* other human beings for hours at a time, or if they worked on machinery that dwarfed them, making it likewise difficult to see and hear other human beings for long stretches of time, I noticed *emotional* and *intellectual* decline. The longer an employee worked under these conditions, the more severe seemed the decline. One other observation worth noting: these employees essentially left their work stations only for scheduled breaks and lunch. They had no function in their organizations other than to be on the job and get the work out—in trade for a check. My impression was *these employees were becoming robots* (Gellerman, 1963). They had stopped growing. The payoff for management was the development of an inferior human being and, hence, an unthinking, potentially inferior employee. Certainly this employee would have little interest in the concerns of management, and my own research has borne this out. If overlapping circles suggest mutual concern of management for employees and vice versa, this situation could be presented by the following circles:

Degree of Separation Denotes Lack of Satisfaction
between Employees and Managers

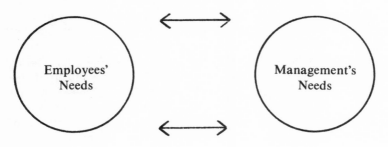

In contrast, in a number of other manufacturing facilities I observed employees doing the same type of work who were much more alert, optimistic, relaxed, and genuinely concerned about the quality of their work and the future of their organizations. When I interviewed these employees and investigated the reasons behind their more positive attitudes, I found a consistent pattern of management behavior. *These employees had been treated differently than those observed in the other factories where the employees were declining.* They had been treated in ways that created an emotional climate which, in turn, promoted a feeling of being trusted, valued, and respected human beings, a climate that helped them feel they were an important asset to the organization. This, in turn, developed a feeling of trust toward management. *The principal management technique responsible for this behavior was participative management.*

Participative Management: Definition and Underlying Philosophy

Participative management appears to be a style of management that releases the potential of employees both to grow themselves and to make positive contributions to their organizations (Alexander, 1981). Participative management has been found to have a favorable effect on employee attitudes and commitment, and productivity. *Participative management can be defined as a way to get things accomplished by creating an environment whereby employees are encouraged to become involved both mentally and emotionally in problem-solving situations which will contribute to organization objectives and goals.* (Scanlan and Atherton, 1981).

Before a manager can decide to utilize participative management as his dominant leadership style, it is *imperative* that he start by taking stock of himself and that he himself determine exactly what *his* needs are—where he's coming from. The manager must *honestly* come to grips with his personal feelings about subordinate employees. He must decide if, in general, he feels they are intellectually inferior, lazy, irresponsible, antagonistic, dishonest, and untrustworthy; or whether they are capable, can handle responsibility, are creative, are concerned with growth—their own and the company's, are trust-worthy, are able to think, and are genuine assets to the organization. If participative management is to work effectively, a manager *must* embrace the latter perspective. He will not be able to fake it. *He either trusts and values people or he does not.* A positive attitude toward people is a prerequisite for a successful participative style of management. Participative management, as a leadership style, suggests the manager feels it is possible, and desirable, for employees to become involved in the organization's problems and in decision making. A manager who considers subordinates as inferior in ability, desire, creativity, cooperation, and contribution potential would not be interested in their ideas and involvement in the company's problems. On the contrary, such a manager usually perceives himself as a member of a small elite, endowed with superior and unusual abilities—the master over his employees, whom he holds in low esteem (Maslow, 1965). Obviously, leaders who perceive employees in this manner have virtually no possibility of gaining their trust and respect. On the contrary, managers who perceive their employees in this respect usually end up having all the problems with them they could possibly ever conceive: tardiness, distrust, rebelliousness, sabotage, uncooperative behavior, etc.

Participative Management and Quality of Work Life: Are They Related?

Observers of quality of work life usually view such things as reduced or altered work hours, flex-time, company-sponsored recreation, additional time off, etc., as beneficial for employees. From my perspective, quality of work life starts with the mind. It starts with the improvement of an individual's self-esteem and self-worth; it starts with helping an employee develop a higher degree of self-regard. *The most promising way to affect an employee's self-esteem over the long term, in my observation and experience, is through consistent personal involvement in an organization's problems and concerns, encouraging that employee to contribute to their solution.* Such behavior suggests that management trusts and values employees, and this valuing of the employee and his potential contributions generally affects his self-esteem and feelings of personal worth in a substantially positive way. This improves the quality of his work life where it counts the most, in his mind, in his personal feelings of satisfaction and regard about himself. Improved feelings of self-worth and self-esteem and improved quality of mental life at work offer enormous possibilities to organizations for employee contributions and collaboration of the highest caliber (Pascale and Athos, 1981). This observation, supported by research (Maslow, 1965; Sutermeister, 1976; Gellerman, 1963; Frost, Wakeley, Ruh, 1974; Ouchi, 1981; Flory, 1965; Goble, 1972), appears to have been little observed by many American industries to date. The overlapping circles below demonstrate why participative management is good business, both for employees and management.

Area of Overlap Suggests Degree of Mutual Satisfaction
between Employees and Management.

Participative Management: A Clarification

Some erroneous ideas seem to have seeped into the concept of participative management. Placing my own practical experience and a review of the literature side by side, the following are some points I feel are worth noting:

1. Participative management is *not* democratic management. Employees are not asked to make decisions. They are involved

only in the decision-making *process*. Only the manager has the responsibility for making the decisions—not his subordinates. The key point, however, is that the manager is very much interested in the thinking and input of his employees, especially in decisions *that will affect them*.

2. Participative management relies on the perception of employees that their superior is not only very much interested in their ideas, but that he can actually be influenced in his decision making. The key here is that employees actually believe they have the power to influence the final decisions of the boss, especially those decisions that affect them.

3. This is not to suggest managers cannot make decisions employees will reject under a participative management style of leadership. Indeed they can. What it does mean is that managers will take the time to involve employees in the decision-making process *before* they make significant decisions. They will take the time to obtain feedback from employees before they make final decisions that will affect them.

4. Participative management suggests to employees that
   a. a decision has not yet been made and management values input from subordinates *before* making the decision; *or*
   b. the decision has *already* been made and employees' contributions are being sought in an effort to find the best way to implement the decision.

   • The point here is that people can live better with decisions in which they have had some input, even when they disagree with the decision. For this reason a participative management style offers to management a device to foster the closest possible positive, trusting, relationship between management and employees.

5. Participative management offers to an organization the most positive vehicle for combatting resistance to change. When the employees are involved, they can accept changes more readily—even changes they may not agree with or like (Sutermeister, 1976).

6. Participative management takes time, lots of time, on the part of management. It will not work unless managers are willing to take time to interact with employees and solicit their ideas, or give feedback.

7. Participative management rests on a philosophy of man that is positive, optimistic, and trusting. Managers who are power-hungry, distrusting, and pessimistic regarding subordinates probably will not be able to develop an effective participative management leadership style.

8. Participative management is not the only style of management but it does appear to have attributes for helping people to grow and for helping to develop and maintain a trusting relationship between management and employees (Wadia, 1980).

9. Consensus management works well in groups of six to eight. It is nearly impossible to attain with groups of twenty-five to forty (or more) employees. It is more practical to come to a consensus decision where there is ample time available and the group is small. When time is *not* available, consensus decision making as a form of participative management may not be the best approach. This is likewise valid when the group is large. But a point made above must be made again: whether a decision has or has not yet been made, employees must be involved in the process either by giving input before the decision is made or by later contributing suggestions as to how the decision might be carried out successfully.

10. Quality circles, from my own personal observations, offer to employees one of the finest opportunities management can provide for rich and substantial participation in the activities and problems of the company. They should become an integral part of every organization interested in employee development and employee-management harmony.

Conclusion

In conclusion, after a review of the literature and my own observations and experiences with numerous employees across a broad spectrum of organizations, the evidence (both hard and soft) points heavily to participative management as the one style of leadership that offers the greatest number of employees a good quality of work life, as well as the opportunity to grow, develop, and actualize their potential during their careers with the companies in which they are employed. Every effort should be made by organizations sincerely interested in the welfare and quality of work life of their employees to look into this leadership style.

REFERENCES

Alexander, Philip. "Learning from the Japanese." *Personnel Journal,* August 1981, pp. 616—619.

Cangemi, Joseph. *Effective Management.* New York: Philosophical Library, 1980.

Erickson, Erik. *Childhood and Society.* New York: W.W. Norton and Company, 1963.

Flory, Charles D. *Managers for Tomorrow.* New York: New American Library, 1965.

Frost, Carl F., John H. Wakeley, and Robert A. Ruh. *The Scanlon Plan for Organization Development.* Ann Arbor, Michigan: Michigan State University Press, 1974.

Gellerman, Saul W. *Motivation and Productivity.* New York: American Management Association, 1963.

Goble, Frank. *Excellence in Leadership.* New York: American Management Association, 1972.

Likert, Rensis. *The Human Organization.* New York: McGraw-Hill, 1967.

Maslow, Abraham. *Eupsychian Management.* Homewood, Illinois: Richard D. Irwin, 1965.

Maslow, Abraham. *Motivation and Personality.* New York: Harper and Row, 1974.

Meltzer, H. and Frederic R. Wickert. *Humanizing Organizational Behavior.* Springfield, Illinois: Charles C. Thomas Publishers, 1976.

Miles, Raymond E. *Theories of Management.* New York: McGraw-Hill, 1975.

Ouchi, William. *Theory Z.* New York: Avon Publishers, 1981.

Pascale, Richard and Anthony Athos. *The Art of Japanese Management.* New York: Simon and Schuster, 1981.

Ritchie, J. and Paul Thompson. *Organization and People.* New York: West Publishing Company, 1976.

Scanlan, Burt and Roger Atherton. "Participation and the Effective Use of Authority." *Personnel Journal,* August 1981, pp. 698-703.

Sutermeister, Robert A. *People and Productivity.* New York: McGraw-Hill, 1976.

Wadia, Maneck. "Participative Management: Three Common Problems." *Personnel Journal,* November 1980, pp. 927-928.

In this article the words management and leadership are used interchangeably. The words him, his, and he are used in the generic sense and include females.

Some Important Issues of Participative Management

Richard H. Card and Raymond G. Taylor

The purposes of this chapter are threefold: 1) to review the issues related to several popular typologies for organizing participatory management, 2) to indicate their conceptual interrelationships through a single model, and 3) to suggest an elaboration on that model in order to deal with the significant element of goal congruency between managers and participants.

There are three broad questions that each manager must address when approaching shared decision making. The *first* is, "How shall I determine, in each instance, whether it is appropriate and productive to involve others?" Then, if the decision to allow or require participation has been in the affirmative, a *second* question follows: "In which *parts* of the decision-making process shall I involve others?" And finally, a *third* question should be asked: "What is the most effective kind of relationship for me to have with those who are participating in the decision?" A substantial portion of the literature on decision making relates to one or more of the above questions.

When to Involve Others. As early as 1938, Chester Barnard, a telephone company executive, made a case for the importance of approaching participatory management in a controlled and thoughtful manner. In his classic *Functions of the Executive*, he presented a balanced case arguing, on the one hand, that active participation is beneficial and, on the other hand, that such participation can easily be overdone. Barnard claimed that there were many kinds of decisions in every organization which should not involve subordinates, especially those decisions which are generally recognized as being in the proper and sole domain of management. He used the term "zone of indifference" to suggest that there are areas in which administrators may make unilateral decisions which will be accepted by subordinates with indifference. Further, if a manager were to ask employees to participate in such decisions they would be resentful and feel that the manager was not doing the job for which he was being paid (Owens, 1970).

Bridges has suggested two general rules to identify decisions in which subordinates should share (Bridges, 1967).

1. A test of relevance. When the employee's stake in the decision is high, his interest in participating in that decision should also be high, according to Bridges. Although relevance must be judged on a case by case basis, there are certain problems which clearly meet this test: working environment, schedule, "plant society" issues, establishing quotas, and developing standards for evaluation.

2. A test of expertise. In order for an employee to participate in a decision, that employee must have something to contribute. He must be competent to deal with the issues associated with the problem in an effective manner.

A third test has been suggested by Owens. Although Owens applied this test to the school environment, it is clearly appropriate to many other kinds of situations.

3. A test of jurisdiction. Most organizations are established on a hierarchical basis. Certain parts of the organization, therefore,

have jurisdiction only over those decision-making areas that are remanded to them by higher levels. The acquisition of such jurisdiction may be either through organizational design or by the omission of others. There are problems which clearly meet the tests of relevance and expertise, but which involve employees who do not have jurisdiction over those problems. Participation by employees in making such decisions will lead to frustration and anger.

Several years after Owens added the third test, the present senior author developed a fourth. Although this final test has been suggested obliquely in the literature, it is of extraordinary importance and should be used in every case where the manager has to determine whether or not subordinates should be involved in management decisions. In fact, the failure to apply this test has led many managers and their employees to a premature and inappropriate disillusionment with participatory management.

4. A test of goal congruency. When an employee's goals are compatible with those of the organization, at least in regard to the specific situation under consideration, there will be little conflict in the motives for selecting alternatives or reaching final decisions. When subordinates work together with shared goals, and those goals are compatible with the organization's goals as determined by managers or directors, then the participatory process not only leads to high-quality decisions, but it develops a high level of synergy within the organization. When the individual goals are not compatible with those of the organization, and that compatibility is not tested or known to the manager, conflict, dissatisfaction, and goal displacement are likely to occur.

It is now possible to develop a comprehensive model combining the four tests and Barnard's notion of a zone of indifference. This model, although rather mechanical in nature, has broad applicability and, in the opinion of the authors, constitutes the most straightforward answer to the title question, "When shall I involve others?"

CHART 1
INVOLVEMENT IN DECISION MAKING

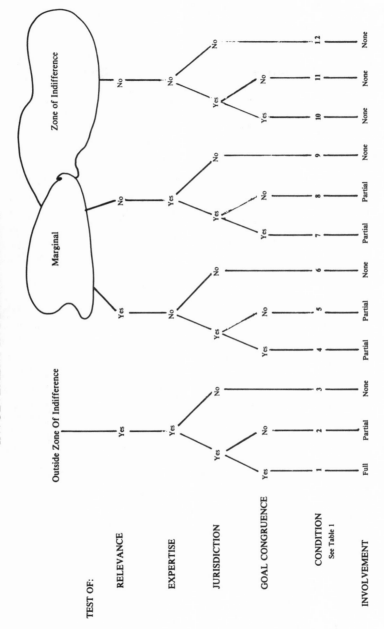

Chart I indicates that when a decision is within the zone of indifference for the subordinate, no involvement in the decision is appropriate regardless of the "yes/no" results of the four tests. Of course, if the decision is truly within the zone of indifference, the test of relevance and the test of expertise should both yield results of "no."

Chart I also allows for marginal conditions. Such marginality is best understood by applying the first two tests. If either the test of relevance or the test of expertise, but not both, yield a result of "yes," then the condition is said to be marginal. In such cases, partial participation is appropriate. Later in this chapter the authors describe more fully what is meant by partial participation in each of the several cases flowing out of Chart I.

Finally, there are those clear-cut cases where the decision is outside the zone of indifference. In these cases the decision is relevant to at least one employee who has the capacity to make a contribution. If the test of jurisdiction and goal congruency are passed, then the subordinate should have a total involvement in the decision-making process.

If the test of jurisdiction is not passed, then no involvement is appropriate. If the test of jurisdiction is passed but the test of goal congruency is not passed, then only partial involvement is indicated.

How to Involve Others. The first section of this chapter leaves the reader with the complex dilemma of determining the meaning of "partial involvement." A good start in answering this question is provided by Hoy and Miskel. In 1978 they published a model for shared decision making which tied three separate concepts together: 1) Barnard's notion of a zone of indifference, 2) the first two tests (relevance, expertise), and 3) the logical sequences of events in any decision-making process (identification of the problem, selection of alternatives, evaluation of consequences, and selection of the best alternative). The Hoy and Miskel model indicates which of these pieces of the decision process are appropriate given the results of applying the tests of relevance and expertise.

The present authors have taken the Hoy and Miskel model, have added the tests of jurisdiction and goal congruency, and have sorted out the definitions of partial involvement for each of the resulting possibilities.

The twelve conditions indicated at the bottom of Chart I are

TABLE 1

APPROPRIATE LEVELS OF INVOLVEMENT

Condition see Chart 1	PORTION OF PROCESS WHICH SHOULD BE SHARED
1	Total Involvement Entire Process
2	Problem, Alternatives, Consequences
3	None
4	Problem, Selection
5	Problem Only
6	None
7	Problem, Alternatives Consequences
8	Problem, Alternatives
9	None
10	None
11	None
12	None

carried forward into Table I along with the authors' recommendation for either total involvement, or partial involvement. In each case where at least some involvement is indicated, subordinates should be encouraged to contribute to the clear identification of the problem. The selection of alternatives will not be appropriate for those who do not have expertise. Similarly, the evaluation of consequences cannot be made by either those who lack expertise or those who do not share organization goals. Finally, selection of a final alternative should be restricted to those who pass all of the tests, with the possible exception of the test of expertise.

The Manager's Role. Participative management does not imply weak management. On the contrary, in order to effectively use the contributions of subordinates, the role of the manager must be clear and strong. The differences between participatory management and that of a more traditional style are philosophy, technique, and goal. The manager who believes that his subordinates have a substantial contribution to make to the organization, who believes that the quality of decisions can be improved by the contribution of others, who recognizes that ownership of the decision yields commitment, will desire the fullest appropriate participation by subordinates. He will employ techniques which set him apart as one who is not only in charge but who has the confidence and the competence to allow his judgments to be appraised and improved upon by those who work with him. His goals will also differ from those of traditional managers in the sense that they will mix production with staff development, task with caring, output with a sound plant security (Drucker, 1974). But these elements of philosophy, technique, and goal must be tied to some deliberate and specific behavior in order to be cohesive and effective.

Although several such paradigms appear in the literature, the present authors suggest that there are at least eight roles or styles that the administrator can adopt in relation to shared decision making. Each is appropriate at certain times, and each can be tied approximately to one or more of the twelve conditions indicated in Chart I. They are:

1. *Solo.* Here the manager operates alone. He neither seeks information nor advice. He will rely on his own experience and his own research, and will simply announce his decision. This

style is particularly appropriate for those decisions which lie within the employee's zone of indifference, as well as any other conditions which suggest no involvement (3, 6, 9, 10, 11, 12).

2. *Information gathering.* In this mode the manager uses others only for the purpose of researching the problem. The participants are not invited to come together or even to know who is being asked for such information. Through telephone conferences and written reports, the manager draws upon the contribution of others in order to make a decision by himself. In the opinion of the present authors, this style has very limited applicability and would most commonly be used for decisions which are marginal to the employee's zone of indifference, or those which do not satisfy the test of jurisdiction.

3. *Information gathering and discussion.* This case is an important elaboration of the second. Here the manager attempts to verify and develop the information by bringing together those who can make a contribution to the information base. As this information is cross-checked and clarified, a limited degree of collegiality is encouraged. The administrator reserves the decision to himself, and may do so with a considerable air of authority, as the first vestiges of participatory management appear in this role.

4. *Opinion gathering and discussion.* Here the manager asks for an interpretation of the information by his subordinates. He draws on their expertise to explain the meaning of a body of data that is shared by the entire group. The opinions may be very diverse and may not yield a common suggestion to the manager for a resolution of the problem. Again, the manager reserves the decision to himself but, in this case, he encourages the free exchange of opinion. This style appears to be particularly appropriate to condition 7, where the individual can be trusted to share the institutional goals, where the employee clearly has jurisdiction and expertise, but where no personal stake in a decision is evident.

5. *Debate, dialog, and equity protection.* In this role, the manager not only encourages the free exchange of opinions, but makes certain that the individuals offering such opinions engage each other in refutation. Through the interactions of the group, an attempt is made to evaluate the relative merits of the opinions

expressed. Because it is particularly important that all opinions be aired, the manager's role includes that of parliamentarian; he will work hard to protect the opinion of minorities as well as those who may be timed. In this role he will still retain the decision-making power for himself, but he will be heavily influenced by the arguments presented. This approach serves conditions 2, 5, 7 and 8 particularly well, and from the standpoint of participatory management, it is preferable to the opinion gathering and discussion technique.

6. *Democratic*. This is the first style which allows for participation in the selection among alternatives. As a protector of the democratic process, the manager will give away most of his decision-making authority. He will participate in the discussion and he will vote. But the final decision will be made on majority rule. This technique is particularly appropriate for highly controversial decisions, where consensus cannot be reached, and where the personal stake of the subordinate far exceeds that of the manager or the organization. Such situations are a subset of condition 1 and apply, for example, to plant society issues such as employee schedules, benefit programs, and social events.

7. *Consensus*. Under clear-cut condition 1 circumstances as well as under condition 4, this is probably the most effective role of the manager. Here the manager encourages diverse opinion and dialog. He acts as a parliamentarian to secure the equal rights of all involved. He provides the time and the personal commitment to make sure all of the issues are addressed as fairly as possible. As the group moves toward agreement he summarizes and clarifies the issues. He leads the group process, but he does not assert his opinion above that of others. He attempts to bring the group to agreement on the best alternative—the one which can be accepted by the group as a whole. This does not mean that everyone will be totally satisfied with the decision, but everyone should be satisfied that it is the best decision that the group as the whole will be able to reach. For the skilled manager this technique will be used as often as possible under condition 1.

8. *Delegate*. Under certain limited conditions, a decision within the organization may fall within the *manager's* zone of indif-

ference. The decision is not relevant to him or to the organization. He does not have the expertise to make a contribution. So, he delegates the decision to his subordinates. He does not participate. He does not interfere with the final judgment. He may, however, be the one to identify the problem.

Although the various paths of the comprehensive model offered above may seem complex, the four parts of that model (zone of indifference, the tests, parts of the decision-making process, style of the manager) interact to describe very different situations. A less comprehensive design encourages the manager to adopt an oversimplified approach to participatory management which could easily lead to discouragement with the entire process.

It is extremely important to ask when and how others should be involved. This normally only takes a few minutes to do, but it indicates which of the twelve conditions prevail. The manager can then decide what his role will be as others join in the process. If he fails to identify that role for himself, he will most likely act inconsistently and will certainly fail to identify his role to others. On the other hand, the manager who recognizes the conditions of participation, identifies his own role and clearly communicates that role to others, is likely to enjoy the substantial benefits of involving subordinates. He will discover the increased productivity and the clear commitment from employees that shared decision making yields. The formal issues in shared decision making should be well understood and should be addressed before any specific techniques of involving others are attempted.

REFERENCES

Bridges, E.M. *"A Model for Shared Decision Making...." Educational Administration Quarterly*, 3(1), Winter, 1967.

Druker, Peter F. *Management: Tasks, Responsibilities, Practices.* New York: Harper & Row, 1974.

Hoy, W.K. and C.G. Miskel. *Educational Administration: Theory, Research and Practice.* New York: Random House, 1978.

Owens, R.G. *Organizational Behavior in Schools.* Englewood Cliffs, N.J.: Prentice-Hall, 1970.

Quality, Reality, and Participative Management

Gordon E. DeMarco

"Almost everything depends, in our perception of reality, on what we think is important. These become our life values." So it is with quality. Quality is many things to many people. This is a part of quality that I wish to explore.

William Glasser, in his book, *Reality Therapy*, confronts us with the real world. In the real world there are rules that we must live by. If we do not live by the rules, there are penalties inflicted. Some are harsh and can result in the demise of a company. In any society there must be rules if there is to be survival. Quality is no exception. If a product does not meet the quality expected, the penalty may very well be the company doors being closed forever.

It is in our perception of reality that quality may be explored. As we observe the many facets of quality from the viewpoint of reality, it is acknowledged that your perception and mine most assuredly will differ. This is reality. Your perception, mine, the design engineer, the worker, the customer—all will have differing views on the quality of the product or service. The most important person whose perception we seek is the customer. It is his acceptance that will make or break our company.

The customer may make a purchase based upon comments of others, or by making a rational and logical process decision, or upon a whim or a sudden desire. There are more reasons, but these are sufficient for us to see that in this real world all of the *ego states*— parent, adult, and child—play a part.

To better understand those who make decisions affecting quality, it is important to see who these persons are and their relationships with others.

Those who determine the quality of a product within a company are: Chief Executive Officer, President, Vice-Presidents, Plant Managers, Department Managers, Supervisors, Workers, Engineers, Technical Personnel, and Secretaries. In fact, every person in a company determines the quality of the product. Most assuredly, some influence quality more than others. But the end result is the total of all who are employed. Each in his particular area of concern makes a contribution to the total effort—the total end product.

Let us start our exploration at the top of the company, for it is here that policies are established and objectives and missions given. The implementation of missions and of policies are, of course, done at a much lower level. But how these policies are implemented and just how and when objectives are reached will be determined by the perceptions of those who carry out the orders given by the top leadership.

John Deming has stated that 85% of all quality problems are due to or the result of management decisions. If we accept this renowned expert's view, the conclusion must be that management is not in touch with reality. By management we broadly include those from the CEO down to and including the workers who make the wheels turn.

It is not my purpose in this article to indict all companies and all levels of management. I just want to show that some management types still are not in touch with the real world.

Dr. Eric Berne observed that people act in three distinct ways. He called these three modes the *parent*, the *adult*, and the *child*. At any given time in our lives we may act in one of these modes. Generally, a person may be more comfortable in one of these modes than another. In addition, most of us live out our lives based upon early childhood decisions which Berne called a *script*. He also told us that interaction between persons are *strokes*. There are both "good strokes'" and "bad strokes." If a person does not receive good strokes he will, most assuredly, go after bad strokes. One thing for certain—we cannot live in a world of indifference. In this, top-level management is no different from any blue-collar worker. All of us require strokes to survive.

So, to understand quality in the concept of reality, it is necessary to know what makes us "tick." At least what makes some of us tick.

The three modes or ego states (parent, adult, and child) are important if we wish to understand quality or lack of quality. At any one time each of us acts in one of these ego states. They can be ascertained not only by words uttered, but by *how* they were said: *gestures, postures,* and *facial expressions.*

An examination of the ego states reveals that the *parent* is mostly behavior copied from *our* parents. This may be a *nurturing parent* or a *prejudicial-type parent*. It operates with certain validity when the information from the *adult ego state* is not available. However, within certain persons the *parent ego state* operates in spite of information from the adult. In other words, these persons do not want to be confused by facts. They know best, despite statistical data to the contrary. As a result, many stupid decisions are made. This can and has resulted in the demise of many formerly great companies. It is possible, however, for a prejudicial-type parent ego state to be changed. This can be the result of additional growing situations and/or a more open mind. For a prejudicial-type person to change is most desirable. It is also difficult.

The *adult ego state* may be compared to a computer. It is an impassionate mode that gathers and processes data. Predictions and decisions are based upon this data collection and processing. This ego state is devoid of feelings and makes impersonal observations and decisions. The adult ego state is rational; it is also without emotion.

The last of the three ego states is the *child*. This ego state is saved from our early childhood and is about seven years old. It is here that love, fear, happiness, hate, anger, sex, and creativity all emerge. The best place to observe this ego state is at ball games and some parties. This ego state can be noted by persons using short expressive words like "wow," "golly," "gee," and "nice." Perhaps this is the best part of us all, and the only part where one can truly enjoy himself. As Claude Steiner states, "It is the mainspring of joy." It is also the mainspring of creativity.

So much for the ego states, but from this we can ascertain in which ego our management is operating and in which manner management perceives its lower echelons. Most management knowingly or unknowingly acts as a parent and perceives the lower echelons as children. "Father knows best." After all, Father is the head. At least, this is his perception.

If I am treated as a child, I shall react as a child. Of course, I might act as an adult, but if this occurs, there will be confrontations. Acting this way would cause crossed lines of communication. If you perceive me as a child, and I respond as an adult, your reaction will most often be prejudicial. However, if you treat all persons as adults, and they respond as adults, the reaction will be most rewarding. For in this mode you and I shall converse in a rational, intelligent manner. You will seek my input, and I shall be eager to give it. Why? Because you have made me feel worthwhile. At least, this is my perception.

Today, much comment has been made regarding the effectiveness of quality circles, which have had such phenomenal growth in Japan. Why was this approach so successful? It would appear that all levels of management were treated as adults. Each person was made to feel his thoughts and ideas were worthwhile. More important, each person felt he was worthwhile to himself and to others.

William Glasser tells us our two greatest needs are to love and to be loved; equally important is the need to feel we are worthwhile to ourselves and to others.

So, if processes exist that make us feel our job effort is meaningful and that we are capable and have an opportunity to be heard—to make a contribution—we shall have a product that will constantly improve in quality.

Management is responsible to the stockholders, the customer, and to its workers. Responsible management must fulfill its needs in a way that does not deprive others of their ability to fulfill their needs. Hence, if management wishes to produce a product that has value, they and the workers must feel they are of value and are worthwhile. In this situation, all shall make a valuable contribution.

How can persons be responsible if they are treated as children? They can't. They must be treated as adults; they must be allowed to develop and participate in the work that is their life. Nowadays, this is called *participative management*. But whatever label, quality circles or participative management, *it is really creating self-esteem in individuals.*

In our real world, shoddy workmanship is an example of not fulfilling our needs. But it is, in fact, a way of obtaining *strokes.* Earlier, I mentioned that we all must have strokes, even if negative, to survive. Well, this is an example of going after negative strokes: poor quality in a product. In other words, persons' needs have not been fulfilled. In obtaining improved quality, we must tap the unlimited resources of employees. By allowing them to contribute, we also are giving them an opportunity to fulfill their needs and to be and feel worthwhile. This results in human growth and fulfillment. Without this, the alternative is stagnation and decline.

Quality is tangible. Hence, we must involve each worker, infuse him with importance, and seek his judgment on the product. Responsible persons recognize the needs of the product. They must have a voice in what action is to be taken for its improvement. They must also be allowed to implement their decisions and be responsible for them.

Frequently, work is defined by boundaries—i.e. a wall, a machine, a department, a district, etc. Management's treatment of or relationship to employees creates a boundary. If they treat an employee as a child, then the employee is condemned to operate within this boundary. Any attempt to escape will result in confrontation. Self-esteem is being pushed down and feelings of worthiness are diminished. Each attempt at making a change or contribution creates dissatisfaction for the employee and others at various levels of work. However, boundaries need not be fixed, and management must face up to this or their product cannot survive. Those who impose boundaries upon others also are fenced in by the same boundaries.

There are management types who manage by injunction and manipulation. Instead of using negative techniques to impose boundaries and manipulate others, we should strike down these emotional boundaries and allow employees to become the contributors they were intended to be.

To attempt to break away from the past is most difficult. Fritz Perls stated, "To be born again is not easy." It is much easier to maintain the status quo of mediocrity than to break the impasse. Do you wish to manipulate others to improve your position, or would you be more supportive of changing the status quo? This is a question whose answer by management may determine the survival of a company. How many can recognize this? *Persons who want to control ultimately end up being controlled themselves.* They ultimately become the victims.

It is impossible to control a situation. We must let the situation control us. To try to control a situation is akin to trying to change a fact. Facts, if they could be altered, would not be facts. So, let us be guided by situations and react accordingly.

If we are to face the reality of quality, we must turn to ourselves. In this, management must accept the responsibility for the fact that quality causes interference in the workers' lives. If one accepts this, then it most assuredly follows that management has the duty to be supportive of employees.

What has all of this to do with quality? Everything. All workers have the need to be made to feel worthwhile and to feel their efforts are worthwhile. Unless each has good self-esteem, the real world will discern the lack of quality in a product. Lack of quality in a product may be the result of a lack of quality in an employee's self-esteem. Lack of quality means the demise of a product, the employee, and ultimately the company.

From Natural to Humanistic/Participative Management

Tom W. Hollopeter

The purpose of this chapter is to look at organizations to see what structures are in place and attempt to predict if they are humanistic/participative, or what we will call *natural* style. It is an additional purpose of this chapter to look at the change process required to move an organization to be more humanistic.

My experience would indicate that *most* organizations are of the natural style. In this type of unit there will be little understanding of concepts, and the behaviors of the management will not be based on principles or theories, but rather on experience. There might be a stated mission, but the *real* mission will be to "get out the product with few hassles." The basis of most endeavors within the organization would be "avoidance of pain"—the lowest of human values. Thus, for a production unit, a certain quantity of product is produced to escape the wrath of the sales department. The sales department in return would attempt to sell a certain quota to avoid the hassles with the financial division, etc.

In pursuit of the goal to illustrate a humanistic/participative management approach, we need to diagnose a natural organization and proceed to the more modern approach. Borrowing from the "focused web" approach proposed by Gary Salten in *Management Review* (1978) and expanding the concept to develop an organizational model, we have a prediction device like the following:

These are interlocking relationships which determine the behaviors that can be predicted in an organization. *How* we will meet the mission comes from the *structures* that will be set up in the organization. These are the policies, procedures, methods, organization, schedules, management tools, hierarchy, etc. *Why* we will set up these structures is to fulfill the *mission*. *Why* we will have this mission will be based on the *concepts* and *values*. *How* we will realize the values and concepts will be the *mission*.

To activate the structures there will be certain behaviors which are developed by a natural process in most organizations or through training in somewhat more enlightened organizations. To put this in perspective, let us move from a model of management for a sports franchise (professional football team) to a natural organization, to a humanistic/participative organization. An organizational model for a professional football team follows:

CONCEPTS	MISSION	STRUCTURES	BEHAVIORS	TRAINING
Winnng comes from quality play	Realize the full potential of talent	Recruit w/Dallas system	Problem-solving	Coaching style
Perfect practice makes perfect	Produce the highest quality play	Have 10 coaches	Assertive goal oriented leadership	Content
Adopt style to talent	Reform and rehabilitate members	Game plans	Using reinforcement principles	Review best competition
Superior talent and coaching lead to victory	Etc.	Plays	Holding effective meetings	Role modeling
		Spring team		Positive reinforcement
		Team meetings	Effective performance appraisals	
		Bonus		
		Scouts	Clear communications	
		Etc.	Est. observable performance measures	

This is not intended as a complete representation, but as the outline of the model. (Note: This would be for a winning organization.)

Now, moving to the model of the natural organization, we have the following as a management model:

CONCEPTS	MISSION	STRUCTURES	BEHAVIORS	TRAINING
Avoid pain	Produce product	Rigid rules of conduct	Functional	Natural style needs no training
Fear motivates	Avoid hassles	Piece rates	Intimidating	
Money motivates	Remove obstacles	Negative consequences for non-performance	Avoid legitimate interactions	
It's the policy	Correct errors	Excuse giving meetings	Ignoring	
	Output numbers all that counts	Exception reporting	Issuing ultimatums	
	Maintain Status quo	MBO	Inflicting punishments	
		Merit pay	Making threats	
		Rigid Hierarchy	Buck passing	
		Best worker promoted	Overlooking good and bad performance	
		OJT	Focusing on outside extraneous activities	
		Status differential	Hiding	
			Demeaning	
			Making excuses	

With deference to Douglas McGregor, I don't really know if this type of management organization has a succinct world view that indicates "money motivates" or "fear motivates." For example, most piece-rate structures include penalties in the "stepped discipline" area if the person fails to work at an incentive pace. This indicates a lack of a clear view.

Most important, however, the clear why-how relationship is not present in this type of an organization. We actually get a short circuit that says behaviors will be based on avoiding pain; get out the product at all costs or have a good excuse. Behaviors are justified because it is the policy. It also produces very few genuine management activities. This lack of management work has been represented by various management consultants and experts with a functional work versus management work bar graph for a total organization. They look something like the following:

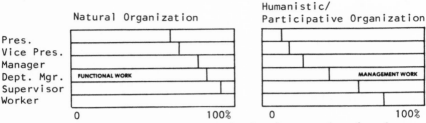

The graph below shows an organizational composite of twelve department managers in my most recent job assignment. It illustrates how their time is spent. This was prepared from self-reports on time-management sheets showing activity in ten-minute intervals, well illustrative of the common problem of too little time being spent on management work.

TIME USE: SELF REPORTS

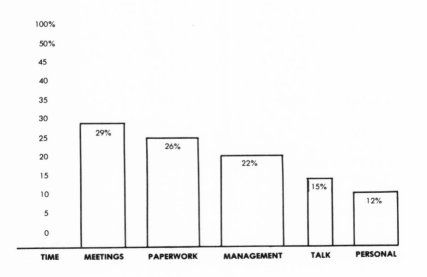

Referring to the first set of graphs, in the natural organization no control of any decisions is left to the employee. The employee is the one to rebel, unionize, sabotage, inflict wage caps, grieve, etc. *All for some semblance of control.* Interestingly, middle management is blamed for blockage in movement toward a more enlightened, humanistic management style. However, the manager is caught in the middle with a functional boss. The details he requires force the manager to remain functional; but, more important, the view of the mission (get out the product, avoid hassles) precludes a shift to a more participative style. This is viewed (participative management) as time that could be better spent on production. Any emphasis on, say, quality would be seen as a detriment to getting out the product.

Below is a copy of a clipping from a recent (June 7, 1981) newspaper:

QUALITY MEANS LITTLE TO EXECS

The American Society for Quality Control recently released a survey of company presidents that revealed most have little knowledge of, or strong interest in, product quality. Instead, the presidents say they are more concerned with productivity, the rising cost of operating a business, and government regulations.

This clipping is rather illustrative of the above points.

So we have a natural organization moderately competitive if the product is not bought on quality, filled with people who do functional work, most of them unhappy and seeking fulfillment through outside activities. Many are locked in with golden handcuffs because this unenlightened organization (usually unionized) pays too much. The U.S. auto industry might be a good example.

Contrast this organizational model with the winning football team. Note that the mission of the natural unit is *output-focused* while our team is *process-focused*. A team, unlike a business unit, has a high premium on doing it right the first time, while in business, for a natural organization to correct errors, inspect its quality, and punish offenders is more the rule. Dr. Edwards Deming is now lecturing and counseling on how the Japanese have adopted successfully his methods of statistical control, and how they are certainly more process and behavior-centered in their business operations than are Americans.

This brings us to a more scientific or humanistic participative approach to management. We have laid the groundwork to indicate that it will be more process and less output-centered. It will be much more concerned with human potential. It will, as McGregor predicted, have a clearer world view of human behavior and principles. Its missions will be clearer and more authentic. There will be a larger percentage of management work being done. Before looking at this organization, let us see how we might approach converting a natural organization to a more humanistic/participative one. Let us say we wanted to institute Quality Circles, which are the current rage of American management. This would be an attempt at a more participative style, and critics warn this is a commitment to change in management style—it surely must be. From the work of Dr. Robert Terry, we can look at organizations from a slightly different perspective than our original model. His model represents management as:

His thoughts, with which this writer concurs, are that in an organization: *mission* directs power, *power* energizes structure, *structure* allocates and uses resources. More important, *resources limit structure, structure limits the use of power*, and, finally, *power can block mission*.

The mission, for purposes of our example, is to become more participative or humanistic. We are going to do this by trying for a structural change—to introduce Quality Circles. As previously stated, when the perceived mission is to get out the product and avoid hassles, we are going to be blocked by power. Thus, most middle managers will not accept or support the change in structure. We do not have a structure problem or power problem, we have a mission problem and that stems from a world view, a group of concepts and values (returning to our original model). So the real problem is to change these views.

To get this change, we will need *sufficient pressure* to change (probably avoidance of pain). The organization's output numbers must need improvement. Second, the internal change agent must be a ranking *line* manager. From our previous discussion, if the ranking line manager continues to be functional, the organization below him will, *by force*, continue to be functional. That means focusing on output exclusively, looking for details and excuses. By contrast, this line manager must be enlightened, want to manage, and must be firmly grounded in concepts.

Next, an authentic mission needs to be defined which deals with *process*, and not so much with output. We must begin to overcome the "get-out-the-product" syndrome. A humanistic/participative mission and mandate might sound something like this.

MISSION & MANDATE

To have contributed to the survival, growth, and profit of _____ Company by managing the _____ so that:

Change is recognized as inevitable. Belief is, there is always a better way.

Enthusiasm and interest center on product.

Hard work is the unquestioned standard.

Individual accountability is fully established.

Standards of performance are at industry-leadership level.

Rewards and recognition are natural consequences of good performance.

Communication is open and two-way.

Participation in decisions by all employees is structured and encouraged.

Conflicts are resolved through problem-solving.

Proper selection and thorough training at all levels are established.

The established management style consists of goal setting, planning, training, problem-solving, facilitation, feedback, control adjustment, and reinforcement.

Actions lead to realizing the full potential of human resources.

Trust is the primary leverage.

As is observed in the last line, the leap from natural to humanistic management approach will be a movement from *fear* to *trust*.

Three ingredients are now present: a line manager, pressure to change, and a correct mission. Now, perhaps the most important ingredient to organizational change is an intervention agent who can convince the power structure that the mission is correct—a perceived expert in human behavior. The middle manager needs convincing that the concepts on which the mission is based are correct.

The natural boss has not had to learn how people operate. He believes he has arrived at his present position because he is good. This is largely superstitious behavior but very powerful. He must be convinced that there are better, more potent views of man and human behavior, and that change is required. This is an awesome task for the line manager bent on change. He needs help. Organizations with which the writer has been associated have utilized the services of a behavior consultant whose views on human behavior, seminars, and processes involved gave a two to three-month window where new approaches could be tried.

The line manager must be a good mechanic. He must take humanistic principles and develop workable structures that result in positive outcomes during that two to three-month period. If we are to install, as our example, Quality Circles, then these preparations must be present. We need the line manager, mission, pressure to change, intervention agent, and finally, the experimentation with structural change. We must meet with success so that this process will be rewarding and will encourage further experimentation with other new structures until our organization is truly humanistic, a process of continuous change. In our most recent situation, we have utilized a behavioral consultant as intervention agent. He taught behavioral principles to middle managers using these principles to overcome difficulties in the participants' departments. Bottom-line results included: fewer accidents, more repair of off-spec material, much greater submission of suggestions, fewer unrepaired products left at end of shift, fewer products requiring rework in the final inspection department, and better, more precise scheduling of components that netted fewer over-age rejections. These results have encouraged managers to begin to experiment with further new projects. This organization is now in position to implement Quality Circles and is doing so.

We have outlined the change process. Now the total concept of humanistic, conceptual participative management needs to be put in one organizational model. First, let us look at some basic differences between a natural and a humanistic management system. These will predict the structures and behaviors we can expect to find. See the model below:

NATURAL ORGANIZATION	CONCEPTUAL OR HUMANISTIC ORGANIZATION
Pay structure complicated	Pay structure simple
Merit pay; individual piece rates	GWI; group bonus
Assessments non-existent or subjective; irregular	Assessments objective and frequent; scheduled
Focus is on outputs, all systems are backend loaded; correction after errors	Focus is on behaviors; investment made at earliest stages; prevention of problems
Rewards limited; output focused	Rewards plentiful; output and process focused
Job training is unstructured; OJT; output focused	Job training formalized; structured, quality focused
Maintenance of status quo important	Risk taking innovative; entrepreneural spirit
Decision making by those in power or pseudo-democratic	Decision making by consensus; participative; democratic
Cooperation between departments, line and staff - limited, competitive	Cooperation fostered
Planning based on short term; closely guarded; seldom considers human element	Planning, long term; participative; considers human element

NATURAL ORGANIZATION	CONCEPTUAL OR HUMANISTIC ORGANIZATION
Organizational structure rigid	Structure flexible; ad hoc committees; task forces used
High percentage of written communication; formalized	High percentage of verbal communication; informal
Large supply of output focused data (largely unusable)	Meetings participative because people know "they can"
Attempts to change blocked by prevalence of I can't statements (to avoid hassles)	Low status differentials; conscientious effort at non "we-they" rhetoric
Large status differentials Perks Elitest rhetoric	"I'll try" or "I'll investigate" heard when new goal proposed
"I can't" frequently heard when new goals introduced	Best candidates promoted based on criteria
Best workers promoted	Communication vertically structured; informal, two-way
Comunication horizontal (peers mostly); vertical communication, structured, one-way	Well defined mission based on developing human potential (concept based); roles and objectives clearly defined
Nebulus or production number as mission Roles and objectives poorly defined	Training job specific to support management structures
Non-specific training	Interpersonal relations based on rehabilitation
Interpersonal relations based on removal of problems	Decision-making problem solving based
Decision-making based on "gut feel"	Authority responsibility defined
Allocation of resources (authority) limited	Supervisory substance, Management task cycle
Supervisory "Get out the product; avoid a hassle" substance, non-goal oriented	Supervisory style varied; soft autocratic to manipulative to participative
Supervisory style autocratic or laissez-faire	Rules flexible; ethical
Rules rigid; non-ethical	Problem situations handled by doing things differently
Problem situations handled by doing the same thing harder	High degree of interlocking objectives; well-coordinated
Departments operated as separate kingdoms; little interlocking of objectives	Promotions of best candidates; interdepartmental
Promotions generally always intra-departmental	

As can be seen, the differences are considerable and various structures need to be developed so these differences are realized.

This brings us back to our first model. We can now illustrate that the humanistic organization parallels very closely to the winning team.

This model is not meant to be exhaustive, but is meant to give some perspective on the process. Just as with our winning team, a great deal of training is required. If we are to continue a change process moving from fear to trust over time by implementing new structures based on a mission stemming from values, we will need to do extensive training.

People will be far more receptive to change if they believe they can exhibit the necessary behaviors implied by the change strategy. For example, in order for many of the proposed structures to operate, it is necessary that the persons involved be able to hold effective meetings. Specific training in group dynamics, problem solving, and perhaps public speaking practice and coaching will be required. Dr. Thomas Gorden, in his book *Leadership Effectiveness Training*, suggests that holding good meetings is the key to effective managing.

Active listening, assertiveness, problem solving: these are all skills which help in producing the behaviors involved in the struture of humanistic/participative management. The strategies of effective behavior management all require giving meaningful, sincere feedback. The skills above all help people who do not necessarily possess reinforcing capabilities. Thus, a very active training program helps when it ties in very closely to the job-specific structures with which the organization is experimenting.

There are other training needs such as facilitation in the participation programs (Quality Circles, control charting, etc.) and maintenance skills enchancement. This might require 4 to 5 full-time personnel in an organization of reasonable size, say 600-plus people.

Thus, if the commitment is to the *process* and not so much to the output, it requires considerable investment both in-house and to the intervention agents necessary to bring in-house personnel up to a competent level. To put this in greater perspective, a professional sports franchise might employ ten coaches for a forty-fifty man team.

What will the payoff be if we work toward the goal of being more participative and humanistic? *All the bottom-line output goals we*

THE HUMANISTIC, CONCEPTUAL MODEL				
CONCEPTS	**MISSION**	**STRUCTURES**	**BEHAVIORS**	**SUPPORT TRAINING**
Laws of human behavior	Produce highest quality	Participative Management Quality Circle	Holding effective meetings	Principles of Human behavior
Morally right	Optimum human potential	Control Charts task force open door	Using assertive goal oriented leadership	Categorizing Management
Trust	Problem-solving and rehabilitation	committees planning session	Practice reciprocal reinforcement	Role modeling
Meets achievement needs		team building		Assertiveness
Pygmalian principle	Product centered interest	Results By Objectives interlocking objectives	Engaging in problem solving	Active listening
Maslow, Hertzberg, Graves; hierarchy; values		Two-way communication open door surveys	Providing reward and recognition	BARS Holding effective meetings
		votes meetings review suggestions	Clearly communicate expectations and responsibilities	Group diagnosis Problem-solving
		Flexible rules	Establish replicable performance measures	Dale Carnegie Panel interview
		Positive discipline	Implant positive incentives systems	Management task cycle
		Formal selection		Pre-supervisor with OJT
		Formal training BARS Charting or Quality based Job simulation Role models	Modeling accountable behavior Utilize panel approach	Formal job training with simulation Value Analysis
		Positive Feedback Weekly newsletter Token bonus system Manager/ Supervisor of month contests Behavior Management projects	Solicit relative creative input Many others	Style necessary
		MBO-go-no go - GWI (General Way Increase) Matrix organization		

now seek. The mission, however, will not be to win the Super Bowl or be the number one supplier of a certain product or to have the largest market share. It will be to get the greatest potential from our human resources to maximize the rest of our resources. Then, overtime, we will win the Bowl or have the product most in demand. Far more important, all the people involved in the organization will have a stake in the outcomes and will have participated in the decisions that bring them to success. We will have moved from an organization where the primary leverage is fear to one motivated by *trust*.

Humanistic/Participative Management
Some Advice to the New Manager

William R. Miller

One should decide early in a career what kind of "style" he (she) should develop in practicing the art of managing. It requires keen observation and considerable analysis, both outward and inward. The style should be a manner unique to the individual, in which he performs his job and meets the objectives he has set for himself—both personal and business. This style should fit his personality, and he should be comfortable and enjoy it because it is what he is. Of utmost importance, it must be consistent with, and supportive of, the organization.

When choosing a style of managing I would *first* read everything I could get my hands on, and today there is a variety of materials from which to choose.

Second, I would study and observe the admirable qualities of successful, respected businesspersons in my company. I would also go outside the company, i.e. business associations, church groups, etc., to find people who possess these qualities of success.

Third, I would talk to people I respect about qualities necessary to be a successful manager. Ask questions, encourage controversy; the earlier in a career one does it, the better balanced a manager one will become. Business maturity cannot arrive too early in a career.

I submit that in the next several decades the humanistic/participative manager will become one of the most sought after and successful leaders. The times today are demanding this trend toward "humanism" and participation to meet the strategic and personnel needs of the business world.

The Scanlon Plan
and
Participative Management

William L. Taylor* and Joseph P. Cangemi*

Of the many programs and plans that have been developed in recent years to increase industrial efficiency, few have matched the prowess achieved by the innovative techniques known as the Scanlon Plan. The purpose of this chapter is to review the concepts and assumptions underlying this plan, especially since the term participative management seems currently in vogue in management circles.

The Scanlon Plan originated in the 1930s and was the brainchild of Joseph N. Scanlon of Massachusetts Institute of Technology. At the time Scanlon was developing his concepts, Douglas McGregor also was at Massachusetts Institute of Technology and was working on his now famous Theory X and Theory Y. McGregor was to have a profound influence on Scanlon and his concepts of management. At the same time, Carl F. Frost was also at M.I.T. and was an associate of Scanlon and McGregor. Although Scanlon originally conceived of this new management orientation, it was Frost who has been instrumental in putting the plan into practice. Working at Michigan State University. Frost has been able to develop the original ideas of Scanlon into a viable theory of employee management and organiza-

*The views of the authors do not represent the position of the United States Government or the Department of the Defense.

41

tional develoment that has proved to be efficient and highly profitable.

The Plan

Briefly, the Scanlon Plan is an approach to organizational development that reflects the essence of McGregor's Theory Y. In his book on the Scanlon Plan (Frost et al., 1974), Frost indicated that it is a philosophy, a theory of organization, and a set of management principles. As a philosophy, the plan is based on the assumption that people prefer to express themselves freely in the work situation, and when they do so, they can be constructive and supportive to others, including their work group and the organization to which they belong.

The theory purports this basic philosophy is best when all the members of the organization participate fully in the activities of the organization and when they are rewarded for their participation on an equitable basis. The principles of management evolving from this perspective reflect that people should be encouraged to identify with their work group, should participate in the organization to the maximum extent possible, and should be rewarded equitably for their efforts. Frost summarized his approach using four concepts: identity, participation, equity, and managerial competence.

Identity

Frost indicates that an organization must first establish its *identity*, and then insure that the process of identification extends to individuals within the organization. The first and absolutely essential step in this process is for the leadership to establish and clearly articulate the *mandate* of the organization.

The *mandate* establishes the broad purposes and goals of the organization. It provides the foundation for all that follows and, therefore, it must be simple, clear, and direct. To equate the organizational mandate to the typical bureaucratic statement of organizational purpose is to confuse the issue. The mandate *is not* the formal statement of organizational purposes, goals, or objectives; rather, *it is the unifying theme around which people rally.* As the mandate provides a sense of reality and direction, management and all employees must understand it and, more importantly, must believe in it. Additionally, and equally important, each employee must know exactly where he or she fits into the overall reality of the organization.

It is through this process that identity within the organization is established and individuals begin to be molded into a cohesive group with a common goal orientation. The identification of the reality of the organization and the relevance of every employee to this reality is a distinguishing characteristic of an effective organization.

At this point one might be saying, "What is new about this? Everyone knows his/her purpose or mission. Why, it's even implied in the title of the organization." But do *all* employees know and understand it; and is the level of understanding between different organizational elements the same? Do subordinates know *how* their jobs contribute to the goals of the organization, and do they feel a *sense of accomplishment* in performing these jobs? Many managers might be surprised at the answers they receive.

Participation

The second requirement for a successful organization is that each employee must have the opportunity to participate in the organization and to become a responsible employee. The purpose of this concept is to create an atmosphere in which employees perceive the goals, and achieving the goals, of the organization as a personal challenge which can be accomplished through their individual and collective efforts. It assumes that employees have a natural tendency to seek self-fulfillment and, when given the opportunity, prefer to exercise some control or influence over their employment destiny. When we allow and actively encourage employees to provide meaningful input into their job, they become more interested, involved, and committed. As a result, they become more responsible and accountable for the quality of their job performance and for the goals of the organization.

Often the most significant suggestions for improvement come not from the engineer, the efficiency expert, or even management, but rather from the rank-and-file employee. After all, who knows the details of a particular job better than the individual who actually performs that job?

Participation, however, must be more than a suggestion awards program, or a mandatory cost reduction scheme. It must be an attitude that permeates the entire organization and reflects the perception that management genuinely cares for its employees and wants their ideas on how to improve the organization. Frost tells us this is not an attitude of giving employees flexibility, but is rather one of *letting employees grow into mature organizational citizens.*

Equity

A condition of *equity* means that all employees have the opportunity to realize an equitable return by increasing the investment of their resources of ideas, energy, competence, and commitment (Frost et al., 1978). Frost relates that employee investment of time, energy, and talent should be considered another organizational asset like that of stockholder investment, both of which are essential to the existence of the organization. As a result, employees are entitled to a real and legitimate expectancy of a fair return on their investment just like the stockholder, vender, or consumer. Frost has developed a viable plan for profit sharing in profit-oriented organizations. But what can be done in a service organization where there is no profit *per se* to share? Can this concept of equity be applied to this type of organization?

On the surface, one would assume that Frost speaks of equity in terms of extrinsic economic rewards; however, this is far from the case. Indeed, the use of extrinsic rewards is only part of the Scanlon Plan, as one of the underlying assumptions of the plan is that employees are motivated by both intrinsic and extrinsic rewards, with the latter being the most pervasive.

Equity relates to a perception by employees of the fairness of management's reward system, and includes both economic (extrinsic) and psychological (intrinsic) rewards (Davis, 1977). Economic rewards do not necessarily relate just to profit sharing, but also to factors such as the worker's perception of promotion potential, chances of a raise, etc. Workers are more likely to be intrinsically motivated when they are able to obtain timely and accurate feedback on task performance, and have participated in setting performance standards (Locke, 1976).

In far too many organizations subordinates often are noticed only when they make mistakes. It seems to be assumed that good job performance is appropriate and expected of all employees. It appears to be forgotten that all people have an innate need for self-esteem and to receive esteem from others. Lack of positive regard from others causes one to question who he/she is and where he/she is at, which often leads to disenchantment and alienation. Although the secretary, the forklift operator, the parts clerk, or the janitor may have relatively minor problems in terms of pay or status, such positions and all that goes with them are nevertheless important to the individuals in them and, most assuredly, are important to the organization. With little effort, a manager who really cares about his employees can devise a myriad of ways to stimulate intrinsic motivation. Often what appears to be the most insignificant act can convey a powerful message. For example, when was the last time a rank-and-file employee received a note from management on his/her birthday or his/her anniversary. In many cases, the employee's immediate supervisor may not be aware of this critical information or, perhaps, he just *does not care*. By just the simple act of caring, we convey a message of positive regard to others that indicates they are "okay"; that *they are appreciated*. It is interesting to note that studies clearly have shown self-esteem is a large factor in determining the degree of an employee's job satisfaction (Locke, 1976).

Managerial Competence

Frost initially saw the first three principles (identity, participation, and competence) as the major elements necessary for organizational success. However, experience with the Scanlon Plan demonstrated there was a fourth principle which, if ignored, would inevitably lead to failure regardless of the effort in the other areas. This principle was the need for *managerial competence*. According to Frost, management must establish, grow, and develop increasing professional competence and effective management systems. This process is seen as one of maturity that occurs when every member of management faces his/her tasks with the assurance that every aspect of the job is rational. This rationality comes from the mandate which provides the framework for decision making and is the anchor that holds the entire system in place. If employees perceive that management is incompetent and that management decisions are irrational, then the resulting loss of confidence will be disastrous. After all, who wants to be identified with a loser?

Summary

A review of the principles underlying the Scanlon Plan reflects that they can be applied to any type of organization. These principles, which are based on McGregor's humanistic Theory Y, reflect that employees are not inherently lazy and will exercise self-control and self-direction in accomplishment of organizational objectives when a work environment is created that allows them to seek and accept responsibility and to maximize their potential. This climate of mutual respect and confidence can be created by the application of Frost's four principles.

REFERENCES

Davis, Keith. *Human Behavior at Work*, 5th Ed. New York: McGraw-Hill, 1977.

Frost, Carl F., Wakeley, John H., and Ruh, Robert F. *The Scanlon Plan for Organizational Development: Identity, Participation and Equity*. East Lansing, Michigan: Michigan State University Press, 1974.

Frost, Carl F. "The Scanlon Plan: Anyone for Free Enterprise?" *Michigan State University Business Topics*, Winter, 1978, pp. 25-33.

Locke, Edwin H. "Nature and Cause of Job Satisfaction." In Marvin Dunnette (Ed.), *Handbook of Industrial and Organizational Psychology*. Chicago: Rand McNally, 1976.

Participative Management and Stress Reduction

Richard L. Miller

John M. is a forty-three year old industrial relations manager in an industrial manufacturing plant in the Southeast. He has acquired eighteen years of experience in industry, including nine years with his current company. Within the past two years his company has been undergoing modification, converting to automated manufacturing. Job readjustment and retraining have been necessary for many personnel, causing considerable unrest in the plant. The union is openly concerned about layoff of its members and is applying heavy pressure on John and his assistant, Susan. To accommodate the demands of the job, John and Susan have put in extended work weeks for months. Both feel on edge, never quite knowing what will be contained in the next directive from upper management.

John's pressures at work have followed him home, where he is having increased difficulty in communicating with his wife and children. He feels lethargic and is experiencing frequent headaches which cannot be relieved by aspirin. Concerned by his physical condition, he has visited his physician and has been told that he is suffering from recurrent stress and would benefit from some stress-management training.

What has caused an apparently healthy, competent adult to feel as if he has lost personal control over the work pressures in his environment? What early signs were overlooked which could have been used as signals to intervene before matters got out of hand? The answers to these questions form the bases for this article.

The Early Signs: Conflict Prior to Stress

John's case is one of many which are seen annually by professionals who specialize in stress management. As is usually the case, many early signs of potentially dangerous levels of stress were overlooked by John as he dealt with his daily routine. Upon closer examination of his problems, one finds many pressures which could have been modified or eliminated had they been correctly identified as debilitating forces in the working environment. However, most people are unaware or ignore the early signs of stress, seeking help only when personal pressures reach critical levels which extract a fee on industry. These costs are staggering. Consider the following figures:

1) losses of 20 billion dollars per year due to stress-related problems, averaging $1600 per employee per year across the work force;
2) mental health services for stress-related difficulties estimated at 14.5 billion dollars per year;
3) disability payments of 10.5 billion dollars per year as workers develop illness or experience accidents under the pressure of their jobs; and
4) losses of 3.9 billion dollars per year from the gross national product due to lost work days.

While the assessed losses are impressively large, the potential for substantially greater losses exists in the noncalculable areas of declining productivity due to poor decision making, increased tardiness, and absenteeism at work.

What is Stress?

Individuals who are confronted by an event in their environment which forces either a physical or psychological reaction have experienced *stress*. However, such a definition is deceptive because, under pressure, many individuals rally to the demands of their environment and accomplish superior efforts. When an individual mobilizes a necessary physical reaction to meet daily demands, he is said to be experiencing *eustress* (Selye, 1974). On occasion, however, the perceived threats of the environment exceed a person's ability to manage these pressures. As unresolved conflicts persist, body responses begin to tax our capacities and reserves. Selye terms such reactions as *distress*. The key factor in these circumstances is the individual's inability to terminate the pressures upon himself. He has surrendered control of these stressors to the hands of those who do control the environment. These controllers can be spouses, company management, cohorts, the demands of a job itself, or in some cases, imaginary fears that immobolize us.

A critical question to be asked of oneself is: Am I seeing an increase in behavior in which I indulge when I am under pressure? If so, I should note these as early warning signs of impending problems. The visible signs of stress are most easily found in physical malfunctions of the body; however, additional indicators can be found in many of our daily behaviors and attitudes.

Stress: More Than a Physical Problem

The onset of a stressful situation produces a dynamic change in the body's physical reactions. Each aspect of this change is designed to maximize your chances of conquering the stressor facing you by providing oxygen and blood sugar to those areas of the body which maximize survival. For example, blood vessels in the brain and deep vessels on muscles dilate while cardiovascular flow to the stomach, intestines, and surface of the skin is reduced by constriction of blood vessels there. The heart is stimulated and beats more rapidly and with stronger force of contraction, lungs increase their air intake to improve oxygen availability to body areas necessary for resolution of the situation applying pressure on you, and available blood sugar is increased to maximize the body's response. In summary, all body processes that are not necessary for meeting the crisis are slowed and survival reactions are elevated. Such a body response is totally appropriate when the emergency faced by an individual can be promptly resolved, but it extracts an enormous toll on the body if the crisis continues unresolved. For example, if an alarm indicator signaled an overheated generator, the employee monitoring the device would be mobilized to immediate action to cut power to the machine. The body could then quickly return to a less stressful state and restore its expanded resources. However, if that same person is placed in a stressful circumstance which cannot be resolved, *he becomes a prime candidate for a wide range of physical problems.* These are genuine physical problems such as peptic ulcers, colitis, bronchial asthma, dermatitis, headaches, cardiac dysfunctions, blood pressure difficulties, and cancer conditions. These problems are termed psychosomatic disorders since psychological stresses induce actual physical damage to the body if the stresses persist. Early indicators of these health problems should not be ignored but treated by a competent physician. In addition, a more important question should be raised: Why have you developed this problem in the first place? If the pressures in your life continue unresolved, the medical problem will recur or be replaced by a new symptom.

Generally, the chronic stress sufferer manifests a broader set of symptoms than physical problems. Persistent stress frequently drives us to adopt behaviors which in the short run reduce the immediate pressures of home and/or work but, in the long run, can prove to be damaging to our careers, family relationships, and bodies. Under unresolved pressure a line manager may become increasingly aggressive, undermining his relationship with his workers. Another manager may experience more frequent anger than she is accustomed to, and in doing so, reduce her effectiveness to an organization. Additional indicators of unresolved pressures are behaviors such as increased tendencies to withdraw from the environment placing tension upon you, a general desire to isolate yourself from interpersonal interaction, general feelings of frustration, increased dissatisfaction, resentment toward others, increases in negative attitude toward the environment in which you are stressed, and general feelings of depression.

Personality Factors in Stress

Within a working environment a common set of pressures is present to influence all employees, and yet a wide range of tolerances to these stressors can be seen. Some workers seem undisturbed by stressors such as deadlines, noise, disruptions, unending routines, and abrasive interpersonal interaction. However, others are severely bothered and find that their work efforts suffer and their personal lives are adversely affected. Stress appears to occur when the characteristics of the worker are not a "good fit" for the demands of the working environment. Certainly one major determinant of this "fit" is the worker's attitude and general personality.

If you are driven toward perfectionism, critical of those who do not perform up to your expectations, chronically pressed by self-imposed deadlines with insufficient time to complete the tasks on hand, you may be a candidate for high cardiovascular risk and a Type A personality (Friedman and Rosenman, 1974). Such an individual is driven beyond the specific requirements of the job and presses for perfectionism in all aspects of his life. Intolerance of performance which doesn't measure up to the Type A's standards may cause extreme pressure on relationships with family, friends, and co-workers, not to mention subordinates. Characterized by aggressiveness and low self-esteem, the Type A steamrolls to success to bolster his own needs for self-approval. Success is measured in dollars and cents and being "number one" at work and play. (Beware, if you are the associate who beats the Type A at a friendly game of racquetball!) Garfield suggests that Type A's seldom achieve their full potential, but tend to work for work's sake. He believes that the workaholic A is addicted to work, but not to results.

The other extreme of this driving, intense personality is the Type B individual. Suffering only one-half the number of cardiovascular problems of the Type A, this person is much less time conscious, although competent in meeting deadlines which he realistically sets.

He is able to prioritize his workload and will not voluntarily take on more work than he can reasonably complete. Working basically for personal satisfaction, the Type B relaxes away from work. This dissipates the cumulative effects of stress which are incurred at work.

Finding the Sources of Stress in Your Job

As will be seen, identifying stressors for each of us is a highly personalized task; however, several common areas of work-related pressures exist and serve as a good starting point for self-examination. Remember, in general, individuals tend to ignore stressors or are unaware of the specific nature of pressures upon them. The following job factors (Beehr and Newman, 1978) can reasonably be expected to produce pressures on an employee in his working environment:

JOB DEMANDS. Work schedules which create tight time-lines, work moving at a rapid pace, a job in which the unexpected may constantly occur, rotating shift work, constant travel for your employer, and high degrees of responsibility for product quality or worker output are all examples of job-related stress. The key to the stress element here is 1) the degree of uncertainty and change to which one is exposed and 2) one's personal feeling of being "in control" during these stresses.

ROLE DEMANDS. In satisfactory fulfillment of job responsibility you can encounter many potential stressors not associated with job demands. These pressures arise from playing out the "role" required of your position. Perhaps your job sporadically floods you with demands for performance which press your limits of endurance, such as the jobs of air traffic controllers during peak periods and bank tellers just prior to closing. Such demands are known as role overload and are sources of significant stress. Ironically, slack periods in which normally productive workers sit idle are also stressful. This circumstance is called role underload.

However, the two most stressful dimensions of role fulfillment arise from role conflict and role ambiguity. Role conflict arises in any circumstance in which a worker is asked to respond to contradictory demands from the working environment. This might occur if you were given two conflicting sets of performance goals, one from your immediate supervisor and a second set from his boss. Which one do you attempt to meet? You are caught in role conflict. However, your situation could be worse. Consider a situation in which you have no clear guidelines for satisfactory performance of your job and no adequate feedback provided to evaluate the quality of your work effort. This is an example of role ambiguity. Such a condition has been directly linked to lower job satisfaction, higher job-related tension, and reduced self-confidence.

The organizational characteristics of your company can go a long way toward reducing or increasing stresses upon you, depending upon its structure. If you are employed in a large organization, you may have a clear knowledge of the role demands of your job relative to your unit or section, but not know how your group fits into "the big picture." This is another example of ambiguity which can induce stress, particularly on middle management personnel. Recurrent findings in the research literature suggest that it is important for the employee to perceive that he or she is affecting the organization. As an example, Margolis, Kross, and Quinn (1974) report that *non-participation of managers in the decision-making process of a company is the most significant factor in producing job-related stress.* Non-participation is significantly related to a wide range of debilitating physical conditions and behavior, among them problem drinking, depression, lowered self-esteem, reduced life and job satisfaction, intentions to leave the present job, and increased absenteeism. Add to these findings the conclusions that employees who feel they cannot openly communicate with superiors, peers, or personnel under their direct supervision are much higher stress candidates than individuals who work in a more open atmosphere of communication. Collectively, these data suggest that *a company structure which actively solicits employee input and encourages open discussion of issues and concerns fosters a healthy working environment in which workers experience relatively little stress.* Further, it is the author's feeling that employees seek the right of input but not necessarily the responsibility of making the final decision. As long as the employee feels that his or her contributions are valued, there is a feeling of personal control and satisfaction which is reflected in both work attitude and performance. The work place then becomes a place one enjoys encountering, not escaping.

John M. Revisited

Returning to John M., we ask the question once again. What were the early signs of his stress to which he should have attended? John, in retrospect, will concede to us that he had experienced numerous physical problems that he had chosen to ignore. He further acknowledged that the severity of these symptoms at times appeared to increase as the job pressures grew. Clearly, John could have been more effective had he developed skills for reducing his physical reaction to pressure in his life. Specific strategies for pinpointing events, people, and job dimensions which are personally troublesome are discussed at some length elsewhere (Miller and Pfohl, 1982). The same resource discusses wide ranges of techniques which can be employed to overcome the identified difficulties. All approaches are based upon the same fundamental principle: Allow the worker once again to feel "in control" of his body and behaviors.

When we talk further with John, we find he concedes that he should have "picked up early" on his change in communication at home as a sign of trouble. He rightfully recognizes the need for a strong social support network within his family to help reduce the pressures at his plant. He mentions to us that many behaviors were there as indicators of problems had he only looked at himself. He cites noticeable increases in short-tempered, angry outbursts, saying that he had never considered using the behaviors as early feedback to himself that things were getting out of hand. John now concedes that he had passed up some early entry points during which he could have reduced his stress reactions and substantially improved his personal life.

If John is really astute, he may now look at us and go for the heart of his problem: Why was he under this pressure in the first place? A quick analysis of his plant spells out many possible answers. With new equipment, former job skills were no longer effective. The possibility of obsolescence or extensive retraining is very stressful. Additionally, a closer examination of the flow of information vertically in the company is telling. Communication moves one way: down. The union personnel are openly hostile to management, claiming no input is ever sought from the line in the plant. Supervisors are used as buffers by upper management as it maintains its distance. As John continues, the list grows and the bottom line in stress management emerges. Simply, a person under stress has limited options. Under pressure, you can attempt to alter the stressors in the environment. That is an unworkable option beyond John's control. He has a second option of removing himself from the stressful situation by seeking other employment. John has ruled that possibility out for personal reasons. His third and final option is to develop specific skills to exist with a difficult situation. This is John's choice and a reasonable alternative at that. But a question remains which is larger than John's collective problems: When all the data point to a minimally stressful environment centered around open communication and participative input, why do companies such as John's continue to create unnecessary pressure on their employees? The question will remain unanswered. Clearly the use of a practical participative management approach can be justified to substantially reduce stress in the work place.

REFERENCES

Beehr, Terry and John Newman. "Job Stress, Employee Health, and Organization Effectiveness: A Facet Analysis Model and Literature Review." *Personnel Psychology*, 31, 1978.

Friedman, M.D. and R.H. Rosenman. *Type A Behavior and Your Heart*. New York; Knopf, 1974.

Goldberger, Leo and Schlomo Bresnitz. *Handbook of Stress: Theoretical and Clinical Aspects*. New York: Free Press, 1982.

Greenwood, J. and J. Greenwood. *Managing Executive Stress*. New York: John Wiley and Sons, 1979.

Margolis, B.L., W.H. Kross, and R.P. Quinn. "Job Stress: An Unlisted Occupational Hazard." *Journal of Occupational Medicine*, 1974, *16*, 659-651.

Miller, Richard and William Pfohl. "Management of Job-Related Stress." In: O'Brien, Dickinson, and Rosow (Eds.), *Industrial Behavior Modification: A Management Handbook*. Elmsford, N.Y.: Pergamon Press, 1982.

Selye, Hans. *Stress without Distress*. New York: Lippincott, 1974.

"Why Workaholics Work." *Newsweek*, April 27, 1981.

Participation as a Method
of Conflict Resolution

Josip Obradovic

For a long time many social and political philosophers have believed in the harmony of society (Coser, 1956). The idea was that different social groups within a society, although differing in ideology, interests, and many other features, have at least a common interest in preserving society and this is the main reason for their harmonious relationship. During the 19th century numerous social upheavals, uprisings, and the general unrest among workers who worked and lived in impossible conditions influenced social thinkers and caused them to postulate a different, nonharmonious model of social functioning. Prominent thinkers like Marx, Engels, and many others started to explain relationships within societies on a conflict model. Their explanations based on real-life examples purported that societies consisted of distinctive groups or social classes which rarely had common interests, and in most cases had opposite ones. And they doubted that different social classes harboring completely different sets of interests and ideology could achieve harmonious relationships. Their conclusion was that conflict between social classes would be a natural consequence of the existing relationships. In some cases they have even viewed conflicts as a means for social development. While earlier thinkers, by emphasizing possibilities of harmonious relationships, neglected differences in social interests as a source of social conflict, the opposite error happened to some classical Marxist ideologists who considered conflict as the only vehicle for social development (Marx, and Engels, 1949).

Contemporary theoreticians favor the conflict model (Dahrendorf, 1962). It is very difficult nowadays to find serious social thinkers who believe in the harmonious relationship model. Only dogmatic thinkers representing particular social establishments do not believe in the idea of conflicts as the natural relation between various social groups. If we exclude from consideration this minor group, all serious contributions to the explanation of social development accept the conflict model developed by 19th century theorists. Allowing for certain modifications, they also recognize other ways of social development than conflict. Nevertheless, the conflict model is predominantly accepted by modern social theorists.

Similarly, global social theorists of work organization believed for a long time in the possibility of harmonious relationships between management and labor or between social groups representing different parts of the production organization (Kahn and Boulding, 1961). Taylorism or scientific management, for instance, was primarily interested in productivity, neglecting workers' needs in believing that wages and good working conditions are sufficient for making workers satisfied (Taylor, 1947). But the human relations line of thought rediscovered once more the conflicts between individual and organization on one side (Argyris, 1957) and between different social groups, especially labor and management on the other. The human relations movement believed in the possibility of achieving harmonious relationships in industry through methods and procedures introduced into organizations by human relations specialists. We have no intention of underestimating these human relations efforts. Human relations represented a step forward in understanding social relationships in industry, banks or institutions. It also represented an advancement in solving problems and conflicts existing within management and labor. Unfortunately, the assumption that conflict can be solved by using only human relations proved to be rather naive and ineffective. In many cases problems were not smoothed over, and they reappeared in the first case when interests of different orientations were at odds.

If we take into account the complexity of modern production organizations, their sharp division of labor and hierarchical power distribution, it is logical to propose that conflict in production organizations is inevitable. But, it is not a pathological phenomenon as some theorists believe. Rather, it is an inherent and natural part of modern production methods. If technology requires some people to make orders and others to carry them out, the latter could not possibly have identical interests as the former and sooner or later conflict will be provoked.

If interests are different, conflict is a logical consequence. For instance, even in organizations with intensive participation of rank-and-file people in the decision-making process, it is logical to assume that some people are future-oriented, and some are present-oriented. Future-oriented people will tend to reinvest a certain amount of net income; present-oriented people will tend to distribute the entire income as wages. The conflict between these two groups is inevitable, of course, and this is just one example.

It is useless to ignore conflict in a production organization. It is shortsighted to suppress it because it will reappear in different ways, or maybe it will appear in the same way but much more intensively. The second time it will be more difficult to handle. Also, it is naive to think that conflicts can be smoothed out by using human relations tactics. Education of the workers in many production organizations is on such a level that they will not accept human relations specialists or their techniques unless their own interests are taken into account.

What methods are then left at our disposal for solving implicit or open conflict in production organizations? All possible approaches can be classified in three groups:

1. repression of the conflict by management;
2. collective bargaining;
3. participation and self-management.

The first method—repression—is frequently practiced in production and non-production organizations, but characteristically most often in organizations where trade unions are not well developed, or do not exist. In such cases management tends to ignore the needs and interests of the rank and file using various techniques to suppress conflict. In such organizations this may look like a successful method for suppressing conflict, and superficially it looks as if solved. But the consequences are long range and sometimes show up in unexpected ways. Experts usually agree that in these cases the identification with the organization and positive attitudes towards it are weak. If identification with the organization is weak, it certainly has effects on workers' motivation. In some societies where conflicts are not tolerated, the identification with the organization is chronically low and consequently there is a general slowdown in productivity. Such organizations claim to have no conflict, but actually the conflict is permanent and, because of low identification with the organization, production and productivity suffer substantially. Turnover is usually heavy: workers and employees tend to leave such organizations believing that they will be able to self-actualize their needs in other organizations better. But in these days the labor market is so tight that turnover tends to be artificially low, so it is difficult to regard turnover as a good indicator of the latent conflict in organizations.

Another way of expressing dissatisfaction or low identification with an organization is high absenteeism. Especially in the countries with developed or socialized health systems, absenteeism can be seen in terms of visits to the physician. All these we can regard as an aspect of protest. Absenteeism, slowdown of production, and visits to the physician represent both economic loss and the less frequently discussed social loss. So, repressing open conflict leads to superficially harmonious relationships in an organization, but if we try to see not only the immediate consequences but the long-term ones, eventually both sides—the management and the labor—lose in terms of lower wages or lower profit or less competitive power.

The second way of solving conflicts—collective bargaining—is much practiced in the production organizations of capitalist Western societies or in organizations where trade unions are fairly well established. Collective bargaining or c.b. has many positive features (Zupanov, 1978). Although it does not prevent the occurrence of a conflict, once the conflict is open it is a very useful way of finding compromise between the needs of employees on strike and the rest of the organization. In many cases c.b. solves the conflict temporarily, although the solution may not be satisfactory for either side. In a way the c.b. system offers a security valve: in case of conflict everyone knows that there is a system provided by which compromise between the sides can be reached. Such a structure, while giving some psychological security to both sides, also limits the boundaries within which the conflict will be handled. But, by limiting boundaries, expectations are also limited. Everyone knows that not everything will be achieved, and that everyone must be ready to make compromises. The negative side is that the rank and file do not actively participate in conflict solving; instead only their representatives (in most cases professional union leaders or experts in negotiations) are active in solving particular problems. The question is whether these delegates are representing particular group interests adequately enough. It sometimes happens that after reaching compromise both sides are dissatisfied, which can result in a new and even more intensive conflict. Some authors believe this happens because representatives of employees on strike are more willing to make compromise than workers on strike expected. The c.b. system is primarily designed to protect vested interests. It is not a problem-solving system which would have maximum numbers of employees active in decision making. The main goal of c.b. is to smooth out problems and to find compromise, and therefore it doesn't allow for a majority to be creative and active in decision making. Of course, c.b. has limits. Problems like physical working conditions, wages and fringe benefits are included, but many other areas, such as market problems, collaboration among companies, internal economic activity, and so on, are outside its scope. Therefore we would say it is a classical union weapon to protect the interests of a particular group of employees from management and at its best ends up in a compromise. It is not a radical method: it may give psychological security but in a very restricted area.

If we try to describe the role of the third method of conflict solving, i.e. participation, we must sharply delineate participation and workers' self-management (w.s.m.) from collective bargaining. There are many distinctions between c.b. and w.s.m., but we shall mention only a few (Zupanov, 1978). Participation means activity of the rank and file in the decision-making process. If some employees are active in the process of decision making, it is logical to assume that they will feel more responsible than the people who are only given the orders. Their identification with the decision and eventually with their work will be greater. They will not feel merely hired to perform various jobs, but they will feel like members of a social community called work organization. In a collective-bargaining approach there is none of that. The representatives of the employees are negotiating and making an agreement with the management in the name of the employees. If we regard participation and its more complete form, self-management, as problem solving of a decision-making system, then it is logical to assume that there will be less conflict in the organization where participation or w.s.m. exists. Participation and w.s.m. are *conflict preventing* and c.b. is *conflict solving*. Of course, there are many exceptions and many problems involved with participation and collective bargaining. For instance, we know that in every organization there is a difference between intentions and reality. Research results have shown that participation and w.s.m. are effective only if there is a real chance for them to be carried out (Obradovic, 1972). If there is too big a gap between intentions and reality, it can happen that not only does the system not work properly, but also it negatively affects the expectations and aspirations of the workers: workers tend to lose interest in the activity and withdraw, resigned to getting only financial compensation from their jobs (Obradovic, 1978). But if participation or w.s.m. is actually carried out (Obradovic, 1978), identification with the organization and one's job is more intense. Workers are more productive and more satisfied. In cases of conflict or a strike in the organization where participation or w.s.m. are implemented, both systems can be useful in conflict solving. So we might say that, although in theory participation and w.s.m. are primarily conflict preventive, they can be effective in problem solving. In many companies that promote participation and self-management there is a firm belief that if participation or w.s.m. is introduced into the organization, one can expect harmonious relationships among different social groups there. As in many other cases, the idea turned out to be wrong (Arzensek, 1978). As in classical hierarchical organizations, in a participative organization there is also a lack of conflict between different interests. But in participative organizations differences are aired during the process of decision making and, if management is not too overpowering in the distribution of power, conflicts can be resolved.

Participation and w.s.m. can sometimes increase conflicts among social groups. If there is no participation, superficially it must look as if harmonious relations prevail. But that may be only a superficial impression. Conflicts are always present when different social groups in organizations have different interests. So, if it is possible to be active in the process of decision making, and if the real activity of many employees is realized, it can happen very easily that different interests show up and conflict among social groups is the consequence. In our opinion this conflict would exist regardless of employees' participation in the process of decision making. It may be more practical to allow the airing of conflicts. The process of decision making is definitely longer, sometimes too long. But eventually, once a decision is reached, most employees will stick with the decision, and feel more responsible for it. If the participative or w.s.m. organization model is present in a particular organization (as is the case in all organizations in Yugoslavia) and if there is a conflict, it can happen that management is dominant. And this has been demonstrated many times in Yugoslav production organizations. But this power is not legal because in the participative model the rank and file are supposed to make decisions, not the management. Managers exerted power, but that power was illegal, and therefore managers were in a threatened position. If such a situation lasts long, a strike is the only response (Jovanov, 1978). So the conclusion is that strikes happen in a participative organization when there is a skewed distribution of power or when participation is not actually implemented. If employees do not have any other instrument but strikes, then strikes will be used. They may be very short, many times only a few hours, and in most cases no longer than one day. Managers are very eager to solve the problem and reach agreement with employees knowing that their power is not legal. Afraid of scandal, they tend to give the employees anything they want, so it can happen that in such organizations employees on strike get in one day what in other organizations (without such organization models) workers have to fight sometimes months for.

Conclusion

As long as different interests can be found in organizations, there will be either latent or open conflict. Conflict is nothing but a method for achieving one's goal or realizing one's interests. Repression of conflict as a way of smoothing out relations between social groups is unreasonable and usually results in low production and productivity or a general production slowdown. Or sometimes, what is even worse, it results in a violent eruption of emotions and protests which are difficult to stop and even more difficult to solve. So the conflict model of organization is the only model by which we can understand the process and by which we can handle conflicts if they appear.

Collective bargaining is very efficient and perhaps even a superior model for handling conflict when the conflict is open and when there is no time for other methods.

Participation or w.s.m. is a radical and ambitious model requiring major social change. It is primarily aimed at problem solving, not the ending of conflict. Because even with a participative model, conflicts are present and occur openly from time to time. The best solution to prevent and handle conflict would be to have both a participative model and c.b. In that case there would be less conflict, but when it appears it would be efficiently handled. Even integrating these two approaches we do not believe it is possible to eliminate conflicts entirely, because there will always be groups of different interests and occasional clashes between them are inevitable. But if such an integrated approach is implemented, the hidden conflicts would come out in the open, the tensions would be aired, and the compromise would eventually be found. Because of their active role in the process, the identification of workers with the decision and with the goals of the organization will be higher. All this should positively affect economic variables such as production, productivity, etc., and sociological and psychological variables such as satisfaction, morale, attitudes, etc.

REFERENCES

Argyris, C. *Personality and Organizations—the Conflict Between System and Individual.* New York: Harper and Row, 1957.

Arzensek, V. "Managerial Legitimacy and Organizational Conflict." In: Obradovic, J. and W. Dunn. *Workers' Self-Management and Organizational Power in Yugoslavia.* Pittsburgh: University of Pittsburgh, 1978.

Coser, L. *The Functions of Social Conflict.* Glencoe, Ill.: The Free Press, 1956.

Dahrendorf, R. *Gesselschaft und Freiheit.* Munich: R. Piper und Co. Verlag, 1962.

Jovanov, N. "Strikes and Self-Management." in Obradovic, J. and Dunn, W. *Workers' Self-Management and Organizational Power in Yugoslavia.* Pittsburgh: University of Pittsburgh, 1978.

Kahn, R.L., and E. Boulding. *Power and Conflict in Organizations.* London: Tavistock Publications, 1964.

Marx, K., and F. Engels, *Izabrana djela* (Selected Works). Belgrade: Kultura, 1949.

Obradovic, J. "Participation in Enterprise Decision Making." *First International Conference on Self-Management.* Dubrovnik, 1972.

Obradovic, J. "Effects of Technology and Participation on Attitudes toward Work." In Obradovic, J. and W. Dunn. *Workers' Self-Management and Organizational Power in Yugoslavia.* Pittsburgh: University of Pittsburgh, 1978.

Taylor, F.W. *The Principles of Scientific Management.* New York: Harper and Row, 1947.

Zupanov, J. "Two Patterns of Conflict Management in Industry." In Obradovic, J. and W. Dunn. *Workers' Self-Management and Organizational Power in Yugoslavia.* Pittsburgh: University of Pittsburgh, 1978.

Developing a More
Satisfying Work Environment

James E. Stirrett

The purpose of this chapter is to analyze and develop a program which will allow a gradual change to a more consultative/participative management style.

A Fortune 500 corporation purchased the facility mentioned in this article in late 1962. During the past eighteen to twenty years, the plant has undergone several subtle changes in the way operations and personnel are managed.

Most of the authorities in this area currently believe that improvements can be made by giving employees more involvement opportunity and responsibility to participate in their work environment. Management's interest, of course, is the higher productivity of labor, while industrial psychologists are primarily concerned with the relationship between the needs for economic growth and human satisfaction and self-fulfillment.

Psychologists have spent considerable time studying and discussing motivation and different types of individual needs. The motivational theories developed by Maslow, Herzberg, McGregor, and Likert have received particular attention during the last several years. In *Motivation and Personality* Maslow (1970) regards the satisfaction of human needs as the key motivators in human behavior. In order of importance, they constitute the following hierarchy:

Physiological or basic needs, such as oxygen, water, sleep, and food. These are the strongest needs in the human organism.
Safety and security, or the need for a stable environment relatively free of threats (e.g., loss of employment).
Acceptance/belongingness, or the need to be recognized and accepted as a group member by one's peers.
Esteem, or the need for self-respect, self-esteem, the esteem of others, recognition, prestige, and praise.
Self-actualization, or the need for self-fulfillment, personal growth and development, and worthwhile accomplishments.

Herzberg (1971) pointed out various management principles and assumptions that he identified as satisfaction/dissatisfaction:

Satisfaction—achievement, recognition, work itself, responsibility, advancement, and growth.
Dissatisfaction—company policy and administration, supervision, relationship with supervision, work conditions, salary, relationship with peers, personal life, relationship with subordinates, status, and security.

It should be pointed out that satisfaction and dissatisfaction are not opposites and therefore are not on the same continuum. *The lack of dissatisfaction does not mean the individual is satisfied; it simply means he is not dissatisfied.*

According to Maslow, the first need must be *reasonably* satisfied before the next one in the hierarchy emerges. Thus, once basic extrinsic needs are satisfied, intrinsic needs assume greater importance (Herzberg, 1971).

In the particular plant that is the subject of this article, the physiological (basic) needs and the need for safety (stable environment) have been provided by the company. In the past several years, the company has only experienced one major employment reduction (layoff), which was for a relatively short period of time. Therefore, the first two needs in Maslow's hierarchy are being satisfied. However, it is important to note that the majority of employees are not satisfying their higher order needs through their employment. The company believes that employees no longer want to be treated like an extension of the machinery; instead they would like to become involved in the operation to satisfy their higher order needs (social acceptance or belongingness, esteem and self actualization) through their job.

The management team is recognizing that employees are capable of managing their personal affairs and that to some extent every employee should be considered a manager. The employee manages his time, energy, imagination, intellect, attitude, emotion, and on-the-job activities of material usage, products, equipment, quality, quantity, and many other items not mentioned.

This plant's overall performance is quite good; and the interest in changing the management style is not a must, but is an extension of the present thinking of the management team. The management team feels that more involvement of all plant personnel would be beneficial to the employees themselves, as well as to the company. The plant management is interested in developing and implementing a consultative/participative management program. This program would place emphasis in areas such as open communication (two-way communication), positive reinforcement, and delegation.

The common denominator for any operation is its people. For an organization to improve, the people must be motivated. In this plant, management wants to increase the contribution of its people and have an effective way of measuring their contribution (not just of measuring capital, equipment, and commitment) and gradually changing from authoritative to consultative and finally to participative management.

At this point, the author would like to point out that consultative/participative management as defined by the plant management team should not be confused with management by consensus, democratic management, co-management, or permissive management. However, it is management's intent that all employees be included in the program and be given the opportunity to share responsibility to influence and participate in the decision-making process. *Participation is one of the very important ingredients in gaining employee commitment.* Management feels such a commitment can lead to less need for the use of formal authority, power, discipline, threat, and pressure as a means for obtaining job performance.

The ultimate goal of the management team is to develop and implement a successful consultative/participative management program. If they are successful with this management concept, perhaps management likewise can establish new, improved relations with the union which would allow the company to make meaningful changes in its antiquated piecework structure and day work rates in exchange for a profit-sharing system which would benefit both parties. Management realizes that a profit-sharing system in the plant in the near future would be very favorable for all concerned. This is another reason why a gradual change should be made in the plant's management style.

Tannebaum and Schmidt (1973) describe a continuum of leadership behavior from boss-centered/superior-centered with the "X" style, where the manager makes the decisions and announces them, and "Y" style management, where the manager permits subordinates to function within limits defined by the superior. The "Y" axis would indicate a highly participative style of management. This example demonstrates that the use of power versus participation is a matter of degree that should vary, depending on the manager, the subordinates, and the situation. The range of leadership behaviors formulated is depicted in the accompanying table (Tannebaum and Schmidt, 1973).

Tannebaum and Schmidt felt the use of power and participation were alternatives to one another, with the successful manager being the one who accurately and flexibly adjusted his leadership behavior to the various situational constraints.

Participation means different things to different people. As the management of this plant sees it, participation applies a system of management in which all members influence organizational decisions. Participation is a matter of degree and it may vary widely in form. Participation represents a modification of the present system, which is somewhere between the X and Y style of management, terms which were coined by McGregor. The participative style of management provides a way of dealing with some of the most negative problems of industrial society: 1) worker alienation, 2) industrial conflict, 3) political unrest.

Vroom (1973) claims that the astute, experienced manager would be able to analyze the relevant factors and decide what degree of decision sharing would be most appropriate. In *certain situations* decreases in the use of power and authority are necessary for increases in participation and employee involvement. The key to the successful use of both power and participation is knowing when and how to use them effectively.

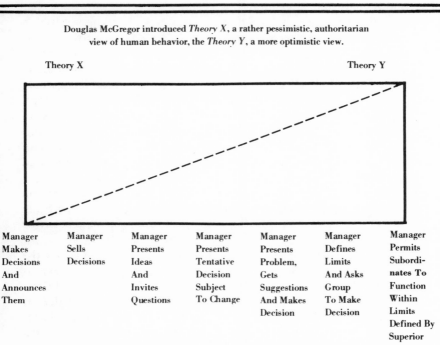

TABLE I
STYLES OF MANAGEMENT

Douglas McGregor introduced *Theory X*, a rather pessimistic, authoritarian view of human behavior, the *Theory Y*, a more optimistic view.

Theory X   Theory Y

| Manager Makes Decisions And Announces Them | Manager Sells Decisions | Manager Presents Ideas And Invites Questions | Manager Presents Tentative Decision Subject To Change | Manager Presents Problem, Gets Suggestions And Makes Decision | Manager Defines Limits And Asks Group To Make Decision | Manager Permits Subordinates To Function Within Limits Defined By Superior |

The increased level of education of the employee in the plant and radical technology changes require some sort of modification of the traditional system of authoritarian, hierarchical relations in order to make sure each employee is involved and develops the feeling of being an important member of the organization.

Rensis Likert (1978) has done considerable work in this area. He labels *System 1*, Exploitative-authoritative; *System 2*, Benevolent-authoritative; *System 3*, Consultative; and *System 4*, Participative. The *ideal* state of the organization Likert identifies as System 4, and by ideal he means organizational performance effectiveness in both humanistic terms (maximum employee satisfaction and morale) and business criteria (maximum output and earnings).

How do you move an organization? Likert identifies three sets of variables: 1) *casual variables* (organizational structure, controls, policies, and leadership behavior); 2) *intervening variables* (attitudes, motivation, and perceptions of all members); 3) *end-result variables* (productivity, costs, and profits). He stresses the necessity of moving gradually into System 4 because a jump from one system to another would not allow people sufficient time to adapt.

He has developed a model of participation that is tied explicitly to the theory of research in behavioral science and is comprehensive in its view of the organization, not its system. Likert's model considers the individual members and the organization. To achieve this type of organization, Likert proposes that each supervisor must form his subordinates into a cohesive group in which he is a member. Supervisors in turn are members of a second group with their superiors, who are members of a third group, and so on, up the hierarchy.

Each supervisor is a member of two groups, one in which he acts as a supervisor with his own subordinates and one in which he is a subordinate along with his own peers. Decisions are made within these groups that apply to the group. Input from the group for decisions which have implications beyond the group itself are passed on through those persons who are members of a second group at adjacent levels.

Likert maintains that an authoritative approach may initially improve changes in the end-result variables (product, cost, and profits) but, at the same time, the intervening variables (attitudes, motivation, and perceptions of all members) eventually will begin to disintegrate as the situation with human assets deteriorates. The end-result variables themselves also will show marked decline. On the other hand, it is maintained that a participative approach will lead to an upgrading of the human assets and, as that occurs, long run permanent gains will develop in the end-result variables.

In the research that has been done on this subject, many of the experts have indicated there can be some negative effects with intermediate and first-line management. If the history of management behavior has been one of an autocratic style management team, a change to a consultative/participative management style could lead to frustration, conflict, poor and/or prolonged decisions, wasted time, and poor performance. It is imperative that, when embarking upon a change in the style of management, a thorough understanding and training process be developed in order to avoid these pitfalls.

Research—During the past six to twelve months, the management team referred to in this article has been actively reviewing other participative/humanistic management styles. This includes reviewing programs within their own organization, such as Scanlon Plan and Improshare, as well as programs of other companies such as General Motors, Dana, Hinderliter, Columbus Auto Parts, Prestolite, Herman Miller, AT&T, etc. Careful study of some of the programs that have failed or had limited success would indicate a lack of the following items:

1. *Support.* Lack of top management understanding and commitment. Many of the companies failed to get support from the top officials of the company.
2. *Planning.* Decision was made to implement a program of this nature and no planning had preceded implementation. In such cases, the probability of failure is quite high.
3. *Implementation.* Most companies failed to provide the necessary training and guidance during the initial phases of the program. The company must recognize this is a change. Even though it is gradual, many employees resist change for different reasons. This must be taken into consideration when implementing the program.
4. *Union Involvement.* In several cases the companies failed to involve union officials in the initial planning of the program. It is highly important that the union be included in order to make this program successful.

5. *Imposing*. Apparently many companies felt they could force employees to develop a participative/humanistic style management. The companies that have experienced the greatest success simply have made their philosophy and the resources available to gradually develop a program of this nature.

6. *Communications*. Many companies failed to properly communicate with their employees. Communications is very basic in a program of this type, and management must recognize that in order for this to be effective they must have a good open exchange of information.

7. *Resources*. Many of the companies failed to provide the necessary resources in order to develop the program. In some cases, if immediate improvement was not noted, the companies failed to involve all employees when necessary.

In order to have a high probability of success, the right climate is crucial. Management must evaluate and be willing to implement changes to develop the climate necessary to make an organization of this nature work in its behalf.

McClelland (McClelland & Burnham, 1976) has done extensive research in the area of achievement motivation. Regardless of how achievement-oriented a person is, if the job climate does not allow achievement or inhibits it, that person will not achieve, at least not to the limits he/she otherwise would. The individual either will quit or, over time, will direct a good portion of his/her energies to other pursuits. Conversely, if a person with an average or low level of achievement motivation is put in the right kind of climate he/she will become more achievement-oriented. Some of the characteristics of such a climate include one in which 1) goals are explicit, challenging and achievable; 2) accountability is emphasized; 3) high performance expectations prevail; 4) performance feedback and positive reinforcement are realities; 5) rewards of all types (including recognition, opportunities for growth and development, new experiences on the job, increased responsibility, wage/salary increases, and promotion) are based on and consistent with achievement as perceived by the employee; 6) support is received in the form of needed communications, policies, and procedures which facilitate accomplishment, physical resources, or sensitivity to job-related problems being encountered; and 7) people have an opportunity to participate.

TABLE II
GUIDELINES FOR MODIFICATION FROM THEORY "X" TO THEORY "Y" STYLE MANAGEMENT

1. Develop a philosophy of management.
2. Provide employees with the necessary training or guidance.
3. Added emphasis placed on positive reinforcement.
4. Improved communication (two-way) at all levels.
5. Delegate decisions to the lowest possible level.
6. Participation in goal setting (MBO/TPM).
7. Review the use of authority; change management approach - employ more participation.

The resulting guidelines (see Table II) were developed and will be implemented in the plant in order to allow a gradual movement toward Y style management. At no time will managers be telling their employees that every decision and every problem will be dealt with in the form of Theory Y. There will continue to be situations that will require X style theory, and it is important that employees understand this during the early stages of the development and implementation of the plant's new philosophy.

Management Philosophy. William Ouchi (1981) has stated that developing a management philosophy is extremely important in making what he refers to as *Theory Z* work. He states that a philosophy can help an organization maintain a sense of its uniqueness by stating explicitly what is and is not important. It also offers efficiency in planning and coordination between people who share in this common culture. An organization's philosophy can be its most useful tool in uniting the activities of employees through a common understanding of goals and values. The management team of the plant addressed in this paper felt an appropriate place to start was to develop a philosophy of management that reflected their objectives.

Toward the latter part of 1981, the plant management team was asked to prepare a written statement as to what they felt their plant's management philosophy was so that it could be discussed in a workshop. A meeting was scheduled outside the plant of all the managers in order to develop their philosophy. The managers were given some basic behavioral science theories and different management concepts *with emphasis being placed on open management*. The group was divided into smaller groups, and each of these smaller groups discussed each individual member's philosophy and then combined the statements into one overall statement embracing all the points considered important. Then the entire management team took those statements and further refined them into one statement representing the entire organization.

During the course of this workshop each member of management had an opportunity to provide input and now has some ownership in the philosophy that will be used by the plant. This will provide a foundation on which to further develop the management concepts.

The following is the final statement adopted by the management team:

Plant Management Philosophy

To create an environment that values trust, recognizes human dignity, and provides the opportunity for personal development and self-fulfillment in the attainment of organizational goals.

As indicated by Dr. Ouchi, a statement of philosophy not practiced becomes a meaningless statement. Therefore, the implementation of the philosophy is just as important as its development and understanding. The management team was asked to thoroughly review this philosophy with all employees.

Training. Emphasis is being placed on providing employees with the necessary training and guidance in order to provide the proper environment which will encourage the consultative/participative management concept. In-house training programs provided by the Corporate Training Department are being utilized. These programs consist of Principles of Management, Intermediate Management, Advanced Management, Managerial Finance, Business Generalist Seminar, Team Effectiveness Workshop, Career Assessment Center Workshop, and others.

The plant is also providing in-house training programs conducted by local management personnel. These programs consist of such subjects as EEO, Personnel, Employee Benefits, MBO, Employee Assessment, Transactional Analysis, Accounting, Industrial Engineering, Financial Report, Motivation, Pre-Supervisory Training, etc.

The plant is initiating an in-depth self-development training program through Dr. Joseph Cangemi, a professor of behavioral science and organization development consultant at Western Kentucky University in Bowling Green, Kentucky. His program stresses humanistic/ "participative" style management, teamwork as a means of improving effectiveness of the managers, and self-awareness to help the individual deal rationally, objectively, and effectively with himself and the environment. It is felt that if the manager understands himself, he will be able to deal more effectively with the people with whom he works. The training program's objective is to improve managers' and staff employees' understanding of themselves and others, and to help them learn about the interworkings and interfacing of the plant and its personnel so they can cultivate their leadership/managerial abilities.

Recently, a new program has been implemented through an outside consulting firm, Managing and Marketing Consultants, headed by Charles B. Alvord. The purpose of this program is to provide a vehicle through which to communicate the mission and strategy of the company to all employees so as to insure common goal orientation.

In summary, the plant's training programs will stress humanistic concepts and gestures, asking for employees' recommendations/suggestions, encouraging supervision that will establish a positive atmosphere, and handling employee complaints regarding the work environment. Management also is attempting to break down barriers with union officials by encouraging their attendance at some of the training programs being made available to employees.

Delegation is a process that makes management possible. Management is the process of getting results accomplished through others.

The objective is to delegate responsibility and authority to the lowest possible level in order to develop personnel and encourage a consultative/participative management program. The main goals of delegation are to reduce dependence of individuals and encourage involvement throughout the organization, as well as continue to develop the team-concept style of management. Through delegation all levels of the management team will be strengthened, allowing more participation, improved employee satisfaction, increased opportunities for recognition and achievement, and improved performance.

Management by Objectives. Management has developed a Management by Objectives program, and additional emphasis will be placed in this area through the positive reinforcement program. The Management by Objectives program was strengthened during the past year with a program called Total Performance Management. This is a systematic team approach for effectively planning and organizing work, for making people accountable for results, and for controlling the outcome of established plans.

Total Performance Management stresses the importance of each individual employee's participation in the process of goal setting and goal accomplishment. It provides a way of establishing specific objectives and a means of measuring the results.

Communications. As the organization grows or becomes more complex and as the work force increases, more is required of the communications system. Perhaps more than any other aspect of personnel policies, the company communications system requires top managewment involvement and support. No matter how elaborate the employees' information system may be in terms of oral and written communications, it cannot offset management that is not willing to share information about the company or take the time and effort to listen to its own employees. Where a favorable climate for communications exists, it allows that organization the opportunity to develop and implement a program that will maximize both organizational productivity and employee satisfaction.

Upward communication provides the employee with the opportunity and encouragement to participate in company and individual employee activities. Some information employees *need* to know in order to perform their jobs effectively; other types of information employees *want* to know because it may affect them in some personal way. There are topics that employees should know in order to be better informed and loyal members of the organization.

The following is an outline of the communication program that will be adopted by the plant:

1. Keep employees informed of company goals, objectives, policies, and plans.
2. Tell employees about various facets of negative, sensitive, and controversial issues.
3. Encourage, if not require, each manager and supervisor to meet with subordinates on a monthly basis for open, honest, two-way communication on job-related situations.
4. Communicate important events and decisions as quickly as possible to all employees.

Overall, managers must understand they have an obligation and responsibility to keep their subordinates informed. This type of communication will provide the employee with the recognition he needs and help to secure his commitment. However, it is important that employees recognize there are constraints. Obviously, information which would be harmful to the company's competitive edge would be restricted. Employees should be told they cannot be given certain information for legitimate reasons. These reasons should be explained to employees.

Positive Reinforcement. B.F. Skinner advocates environment-inquiring to change behavior. He is the author of *Beyond Freedom and Dignity* (Skinner, 1978). He contends that to change behavior, to make an employee more productive, the environment must be manipulated. A fundamental Skinnerian principle is that behavior can be engineered, shaped, or changed by a carefully controlled system of rewards—a process he calls positive reinforcement. In an industrial setting, this is accomplished by telling an employee regularly how well he is meeting objectives and rewarding performance involvement. This can be handled through praise and recognition.

Skinner believes that punishment for such things as poor performance can only produce negative results.

It is also noteworthy that Maslow, Herzberg, and McGregor each felt that achievement, praise, and recognition played an important part in job satisfaction.

Several programs are in the process of development that will be implemented in the plant:

1. A positive reinforcement program similar to that utilized by Emery Air Freight Company, where each employee measures his own performance and reviews the results with his superiors. Management will give praise or recognition to any improvements regardless of how slight they may be.
2. Job-posting program for employees. This will allow employees to be aware of positions that could offer promotional opportunities.
3. Employees will be given additional information regarding merit compensation, grade level, and grade level pay ranges.
4. Employees will have complete access to all information in their personnel file.
5. Employees will be given the opportunity to read, sign, and comment on their employee assessment.

Conclusion

The consultative/participative management approach provides a way for employees to obtain satisfaction, involvement, and recognition from their employment. Through this approach the company can link positive reinforcement, communication, delegation, management by objectives, job enrichment, productivity, and profit improvement into a practical program that pays dividends for both the employee and the organization.

REFERENCES

Herzberg, Frederick. "Managers or Animal Trainers." *Management Review*, Vol. 60, No. 7, July 1971.

Likert, Rensis. *Effective Management and the Behavioral Sciences*. In William Dowling (Ed.), AMACOM, 1978.

Maslow, Abraham. *Motivation and Personality*. New York: McGraw-Hill Book Company, Inc., 1970, Chapter 8.

McClelland, David C. and Burnham, David H. "Power Is A Great Motivator." *Harvard Business Review*, March-April 1976, p. 110.

Ouchi, William. *Theory Z*. Reading, Mass.: Addison-Wesley Publishing Company, 1981.

Skinner, B.F. *Effective Management and the Behavioral Sciences*. In William Dowling (Ed.), AMACOM, 1978.

Tannebaum, Robert and Schmidt, Warren H. "How to Choose A Leadership Pattern." *Harvard Business Review*, May-June 1973.

Vroom, Victor H. "A New Look At Managerial Decision Making." *Organizational Dynamics*, Vol. 1, No. 4, Spring 1973.

A Banker's Perspective on Participative Management

Richard Alan Potter

The management of employees has been of great concern to leaders since there has been a need for human effort to be coordinated and directed. Moses was given management advice by his father-in-law when he was having problems accomplishing tasks which required the efforts of many people. He was advised to identify individuals who had abilities to direct the efforts of a few and give them the responsibility to direct "middle managers." Those middle managers were then given the responsibility for others. Moses also received instructions on how to establish chains of command from the lowest officer to the highest general in the army. All of the advice given to Moses related to the structure of a chain of command. It did not refer to the motivation of those who were being managed.

Recent management study has shifted from an emphasis on structure to a concentration on motivation and humanistic/participative management. Managers understand that they must consider motivating factors and the needs and desires of their employees in order to achieve the goals of the organization. The structure of the organization has been studied and discussed in many business and banking books, articles, and papers during the past several years. Consequently, this article does not concern itself with structure, but concentrates on the human element in management.

Banking is a service industry. As such, it is heavily dependent upon its employees to provide efficient and profitable service to customers. Individual banks are financial intermediaries which offer a wide range of financial services, but these banks usually offer basic services which are almost identical. They normally offer the same kind of loans, such as real estate, commercial, and consumer loans. Competition usually forces the interest rates charged on the same type of loan, the closing costs charged in connection with the loan, and the maximum number of months allowed for repayment of the loan to be similar. These three factors determine the total cost to the consumer as well as the monthly payment amount. Since the customer is mostly interested in his total cost and his monthly payment, competition among bankers generally causes the interest rate and term of the loan to be similar, if the banks are competing for the same customers. The categories of deposits available to customers are also similar. The checking accounts, NOW accounts, savings accounts, and certificate of deposit offerings are normally similar. The interest rates paid on deposits are similar and service charges to customers on checking accounts are also competitive. Banks also provide many other financial services which are similar in the benefit and cost to the customer, such as trust services, wire transfers, investment counseling, international banking services, data processing, and many other services.

The similarities in the services which are offered by banks was explained to emphasize the importance of the people who work in the banks and the attitude of management toward the employees. Banks are identified and differentiated in large part by the ways in which the similar services are provided to the customers by the bank's contact employees. The relative success of each individual bank depends upon the manner in which the employees of the bank perform their responsibilities. The bank whose employees are the most proficient, efficient, enthusiastic, timely, and courteous in providing the services offered by the bank will be the most successful. The bank's goals relating to growth and profitability will be more likely to be met if the employees work toward achieving them. Most bank managers understand that the future success of the bank will depend upon the employees and that competitive, highly motivated, and efficient employees mean higher profits to the bank. The major problem for all management is how to motivate employees to be more effective.

Another major problem relates to the difficulty of a service company, such as a bank, in measuring the productivity of an individual employee. Individual productivity of an employee in a manufacturing business is usually measured by unit output, while quality of work is indicated by the number of production units rejected by quality control. The greater the output and the lower the reject rate, generally, the greater the value of an employee to a company. The productivity of a bank employee is more difficult to determine. The value of an individual to a bank is a combination of his actual work output and his effectiveness as a customer contact person. A very high percentage of a bank's employees come into direct contact with the bank's customers. The satisfaction of the customer is, therefore, a combination of the services he receives from the bank product and the intrinsic satisfaction of dealing with a specific individual. If a customer feels he is dealing with an efficient and courteous bank employee who is sincerely interested in the customer, then he will continue to do business with the bank. A loyal bank customer also attracts other customers to his bank. A dissatisfied customer can cause a bank to lose present customers, as well as lose the opportunity to attract new clients. The personal contact between employee and customer makes people management and motivation very important. Employees must become motivated to attract new customers to the bank and refer existing customers to other services available.

Many bank managers realize how important people are to the customers of the bank and have begun using participative management as a tool to motivate employees to do their best in their jobs in order to satisfy their individual goals and become as productive as possible for their bank. Employee morale and individual incentive for personal job satisfaction are very important to the bank, and more managers are understanding the importance of these factors. Individual goals and bank goals become complimentary and easier to attain with participative management.

Participative/humanistic managers are concerned about the individual employee. They assist and encourage each employee to work toward maximizing his potential. The humanistic manager encourages employees to continue their education in order to enhance their individual development and grow in their careers. As an employee develops, he becomes more valuable to the bank and his career advancement progresses. Employees who believe that their supervisors are concerned with their well-being and future have higher morale and become more productive employees for the bank. The employees begin to believe they are working for their own long-term benefit. They are positive in their attitudes toward the bank and transmit those positive feelings to their customers.

Encouraging an employee to perform well and to continue his development gives the employee a feeling "the bank" cares about him and considers him to be a valuable employee. Most individuals have good feelings relating to the contributions they make to their employers. When a manager or supervisor also shows concern about an employee, the employee is reinforced in his own positive opinion of himself and tries even harder to provide a valuable contribution to the bank. Humanistic managers understand that the best way to receive maximum performance from each employee is to *encourage* him—not drive him. Humanistic/participative managers motivate positively, not negatively.

Motivation in a bank's lending department is sometimes very difficult. A progressive bank that is attempting to achieve high growth goals will attempt to stimulate growth in the loan departments. An individual loan officer may then be faced with conflicting goals. On the one hand, he may be encouraged to be aggressive (liberal) in his lending. On the other hand, the conflict occurs when he is also required to maintain high quality and safety in his loan portfolio. Credit judgments are required when granting loans. A program to increase the total loan portfolio can lead to a reduction in loan quality.

Normally, the major way for one bank in an otherwise stable environment to increase its share of the loans within that environment is to relax its credit standards. When credit standards are relaxed the loan-loss ratio in the bank will increase. The almost certain increase in the loan-loss ratio is not necessarily an unacceptable by-product of a relaxation of the credit standards if the relaxation is a strategy to attain a specific goal and is temporary. The increase in the loan portfolio will result in higher interest and loan fee revenue and these increased loan revenues may offset the increase in loan losses. It is assumed that most of the new loans granted from this initial relaxation of credit standards and reduction of interest will motivate new customers to remain customers after the bank returns to normal credit standards and interest rates.

The bank's loan officers may be unnecessarily pressured by the opposing goals. The humanistic/participative manager will not demand the conflicting goals of an increase in the loan portfolio corresponding with a stable loan quality or an improvement in loan quality. He understands the trade-off between loan growth and loan quality. He also understands that in order to attract a new customer to the bank, it will be necessary to spend more time with the potential new customer.

Employees want to be as informed as possible. They want to know what is expected of them, what changes are contemplated as far in advance as possible, and what management thinks their future with the bank will be. In many instances, an employee is given very vague data as to what is expected of him, and inadequate training as to how he should perform his job. The bank's and department's specific goals should be identified to everyone who is expected to contribute toward these goals, while the individual's specific responsibility toward the achievement of the bank's and the department's goals should be made clear to every employee. The expectations also should be put in numerical form. For example, "A loan officer's new customer development responsibility during a specific time period is to generate $2,000,000 in new loans of a good quality [define "good quality"] while maintaining a 3% delinquency rate in his current loan portfolio and not lose any of his present customers identified as good quality and above." If a loan officer is measured only by the new customers he attracts to the bank, then he may neglect his present customers and cause them to change banks. This potential problem impact could negate the positive effect of any new customers who come into the bank. The above-stated goal is specific and understandable. The loan officer and manager periodically can monitor progress toward the achievement of this specific goal. This is just one example of many goals which every individual loan officer should be working toward fulfilling.

Incentive goals to increase loans in a bank must be very carefully defined and monitored. There have been many instances where a program to increase loans in a bank has had negative impacts on the annual profits and quality of the bank. It is easy to increase the loan portfolio of an individual loan officer or loan department. Simply, grant loans to otherwise uncreditworthy customers or reduce loan interest rates to very low levels. These methods of increasing the loan portfolio are contrary to the original goal of increasing bank profits through activities within the loan department.

The same kinds of conflicts also can occur when attempting to increase deposits. The easiest way to increase deposits is to pay a higher interest rate on certificates of deposit. The interest rates paid on certificates of deposit of $100,000 or more are not restricted by any bank regulation. If the only goal of bank management is to increase deposit, then higher interest rates on those certificates of deposit can be paid. Top managers who are humanistic managers cannot, and do not, give this kind of goal to their subordinate managers who are responsible for deposit growth. This kind of goal would conflict with the bank's profit goals.

Participative managers assume each employee is dedicated to the organization, wants to make an honest, effective, and positive contribution to the organization, and is attempting to improve his ability to perform his duties and responsibilities. The employees need, however, encouragement, appreciation, and total understanding of what is expected of them. Participative managers praise each employee who does exceptional work; they do not offer "false" praise for work which is only adequate. The humanistic manager understands that unworthy praise produces few positive results and may produce negative performance. If a barely adequate performer, who is capable of doing better, receives praise, then he will in all probability assume that what he is doing is appropriate and will continue to perform in that manner. He is not motivated to do better if he believes that his performance is worthy of praise. The high-producing employee also may resent an adequate performer receiving praise or not being reprimanded when necessary. His resentment may cause him to reduce his performance. The humanistic manager recognizes the above and will encourage the poor or adequate performer to improve. He will save his praise for the employee who realistically deserves it.

The humanistic manager also understands that occasionally he will be called upon to terminate the employment of an individual who cannot or will not do what is required of him. The humanistic manager initially will attempt to help an employee correct his performance and encourage him to take the necessary corrective actions. If the efforts to improve the performance of an underproductive employee are not successful, then it is recognized that the employee must be terminated. That is the only fair recourse for the manager and the other employees. The humanistic manager characteristically tries to do what is best for each individual employee, but he is in a management position in the bank and also must act in the best interest of the organization as a whole. No department can expect to attract and keep only the best people, but the humanistic manager rightfully expects his employees to attempt to improve and continue their learning.

The humanistic manager understands that keeping an underproductive employee has at least two negative impacts on the operations of a bank. A productive employee provides more output than an underproductive or poor employee. An unproductive employee costs a business in pay and benefits as much as a productive one. If he is retained at the bank, then the profits of the bank are negatively impacted. The goals of neither the department nor the bank as a whole will be achieved with an underproducer as an employee.

A productive employee also may lose his incentive to provide superior performance for his bank if he sees an underproducer being retained by the department in the bank. He could feel resentment toward the manager and the department's morale may decline. He could say, "He doesn't work but the bank keeps him so why should I work hard," or, "She comes in late every day and our manager doesn't seem to care, so why shouldn't I sleep a little longer in the morning?" There is a great temptation for some employees to reduce their efforts if they feel that management is being unreasonably lenient with underproducers. One "bad apple" may have a negative impact on everyone in the department and cause the department to fail to meet its goals. When one department fails to meet its goals it will be more difficult for the entire bank to meet its goals.

Participative management should not be confused with a loose, open, unstructured, employee-decision type management which allows an employee to set his own limits. Some managers are very demanding of their employees. They expect superior performance from themselves and from everyone else in the organization. Many employees in every kind of organization are capable of superior performance, but perform in an average or poor manner because they have never been motivated or encouraged to excel.

Employees tend to work with the same enthusiasm and drive they observe in their supervisors. Departments reflect the personalities of their managers. If the manager is not highly motivated and does not expect excellence from himself, then his employees probably will not be motivated to excel either. That same department can "come alive" and become much more productive if a more motivated manager comes to the department. A demanding supervisor who expects his employees to provide more work of higher quality *can achieve those results*. Some employees become surprised at what they can do. Most people make contributions well below their abilities and will be very appreciative of the new encouragement and guidelines they receive. They may always have been willing to work hard and provide increased productivity for their department, but in many cases they may not have been asked to provide better work for their bank. We often are surprised at what we can do when we ask ourselves to do something, and at what other people can do when we ask them. Participative managers usually ask more, not less, from their employees.

Many managers feel compelled to dictate the actions of their subordinates. They are given responsibility to manage a specific area or department in the bank and are expected to provide positive results from that department toward meeting the bank's goals and objectives. The manager knows what is expected of him and realizes that higher management looks to him when they measure the performance of his subordinates. He must see to it that his department performs well. He will be rewarded for good performance and not rewarded for poor performance. If his department does not perform what is expected of it, then the manager's advancement may be restricted.

A Theory X manager may decide the best way to attain the goals which have been assigned to him is to control very carefully the actions of his subordinates. He feels he must make all decisions, plan all activities within the department, and very carefully monitor the work assigned to and performed by each of his employees. After all, he is the person to whom top management is looking for the successful performance of his department.

This type of logic is defensible on the surface, but a more thorough examination of this close control type of management reveals the weaknesses associated with too much managing. Junior bank officers and employees have little incentive or opportunity to grow professionally. Participative managers recognize the need of the individual to continue to develop, so they give their subordinates more decision-making responsibilities. When the subordinate makes decisions on his own he develops more quickly and takes some of the pressure off the manager. The manager has more time to concentrate on planning, setting objectives, and other activities if he allows his subordinates to make most necessary decisions. Management succession from within is also stifled unless junior executives and employees are allowed to make decisions as they grow and learn from their mistakes. Participative managers also realize that delegation of responsibilities gives the manager the opportunity to perform more work.

Employees are, as a whole, interested in improving their own personal development and performance. They recognize that, as they grow and become more efficient, so does the bank. As the employee does better, the bank does better and the employee receives rewards. Humanistic managers reward the employee who improves himself educationally because they also recognize that as the employee becomes more efficient, the bank's performance improves. At least the potential for improvement is enhanced. Education in the form of classroom instruction, seminars, and other specialized schools, in addition to specific on-the-job training, helps the employee become better trained to fulfill his and the bank's goals. When bank management develops career paths for an individual employee the employee can concentrate on specific education to become better suited to the progression up his career path. An employee should determine his special interests and concentrate his educational interests in those areas. Someone who is interested in accounting should take courses in accounting, and someone who has a special interest in investments should concentrate his educational efforts in investments, provided these interests are consistent with the bank's needs and career thoughts relating to him. The humanistic manager recognizes the value in career planning to the organization and the employees within it, and attempts to use career planning in his long range planning for the bank.

The surveys which have been taken to demonstrate what employees want from their jobs, compared with what managers *think* employees want from their jobs, are applicable to banking as well as other businesses. Managers have been told what employees, as a whole, want from their jobs, but some have not learned or believed what they have been told about employee wants. It seems inconceivable that anyone who has studied management theory has not been exposed to the following graph of employee expectations (*Success Unlimited*, January 1981, p. 17):

What Managers Think Employees Want		What Employees Really Want
1	Good Pay	5
2	Job security	4
3	Promotion and growth	6
4	Good working conditions	7
5	Interesting work	1
6	Tactful discipline	10
7	Loyalty to employees	8
8	Full appreciation of work done	2
9	Help with personal problems	9
10	Feeling of being in on things	3

Humanistic managers take these studies seriously and attempt to adjust their thinking to reflect employee expectations. They genuinely want to do what they can to help employees get more satisfaction from their jobs. They do what they can to make jobs more interesting and challenging, try to show appreciation for the efforts of the employees, and try to keep employees as informed as possible. When these three top priority items are concentrated upon, the more obvious areas of good pay and job security are more positively emphasized to the employees.

When the management of a bank, or any other business, sets goals for their organization, the goals invariably relate to profit, growth, customer attraction, or possibly new products or services to offer to present and potential customers. Business executives spend long hours discussing and planning ways to improve the numbers in business. They always want to increase profits or the assets of the business. These are the most traditional goals of all business. They want more customers and to develop new ways or products to attract those customers. If those customers are attracted, the management then concentrates on increasing production to meet the increased demand.

The concentration by management on the numbers in business is understandable because *success is measured in numbers*. The bank which experiences the most growth in assets or profits is thought of as the most successful. The rates of return on capital and assets are ratios which are always studied to determine the relative financial strength of the bank or other business. These numbers are very important to a bank, but managers must understand that in order to achieve the traditional goals of an organization it is also necessary to set "people" goals and concentrate on accomplishing these goals. When the goals which relate to the satisfaction of employees are met, the goals of the organization are more easily accomplished because the organization has more enthusiastic and capable employees working toward accomplishing the goals.

Managers are becoming more aware of a need to concentrate on the needs, concerns, feelings, emotions, and ambitions of their employees. Most banks provide acceptable wages, job security, and advancement potential for the majority of their employees, but in many instances fail in some of the other areas of concern to their employees. Bank managements have been relatively successful in the top three areas of concern identified by the chart because they have concentrated on those areas. When managers of all kinds of businesses recognize the importance of concentrating on the areas of importance identified by employees, then they can become more successful because the employees will become more interested in their jobs and consequently more productive. A happy, interested, growth-oriented, and motivated employee becomes a more productive employee and helps the business more easily achieve its goals. Employees who are well trained, well managed, and organized make their businesses more successful.

A bank which has a large proportion of its employees as customer contact employees should be more directly affected by the employees' feelings toward themselves and their management. When the workers feel good about themselves and their bank, they are more likely to present a good image to the public. Consequently, when employees have negative feelings toward customers, they are not likely to show an interest in the customer or make a real effort to assist a customer solve a problem. They become more superficial in their dealings with customers and the customers can easily perceive the lack of genuine concern toward them. Customers do not feel loyal to a bank whose employees are not interested in them. The people who work in a bank make the difference between portraying a warm, concerned bank or a cold, unconcerned one.

There are many things that managers can do to make employees feel more important to the organization and help both the employees and the organization achieve its goals. The goals of the employee and the organization can then become complementary and not be in conflict. Everyone in the organization can become more satisfied when there exists a mutual understanding between management and employees.

There are many specific ways for managers to develop a better line of communication in order to become better managers. Among them are:

1. *Develop open lines of communication with employees.* They have good ideas and will discuss them if management indicates a willingness to listen. Good ideas do not always come from the top.
2. *Identify goals of the business as a whole, the department, and the individual.* Everyone wants to know what is expected of him. When expectations are specifically identified to employees they are more likely to perform as expected. Create individual goals which are common with the goals of the company.

3. *Keep employees well-informed.* When changes are expected by employees, they are more easily implemented and the intended results are more likely to occur. Everyone is concerned about his future with the bank.

4. *Be honest.* Tell the truth to everyone in the organization—even if it is unpleasant. Employees can tell when managers are not being honest, and eventually the truth becomes evident any way. Employees trust managers who are honest and sincere and, conversely, they do not trust managers who are dishonest. We all work better for people we trust.

5. *Empathize with employees.* Make a real effort to understand how the employee feels and how he perceives a problem. Then consider the feelings of employees when making decisions. Managers cannot always make decisions just as the employees want, but employees feel better toward managers when they know their feelings or ideas have been considered.

6. *Stay on top of problems.* When problems are solved quickly their negative impacts are reduced. Managers should:
   a. Perceive that a problem exists.
   b. Identify the specific problem.
   c. Solve it as quickly as possible.

7. *Tell employees they are important to the organization and they are needed.* If good employees feel important and needed, then they want to cooperate with their managers and they become more effective.

8. *Provide employees with educational opportunities.* They can become better informed and more highly trained. They then are more likely to become better, more productive employees.

9. *Develop career paths for employees.* This kind of a long range plan provides a more specific target for the employee to work toward. He can train for a specific goal. He also feels more permanently a part of the organization.

10. *Listen!* Employees will offer suggestions if they believe management will listen to their ideas and use them if they offer a better alternative to present practices. They will continue to think. All of the ideas suggested by the employees will probably not be unique and useful, but they should all be considered.

11. *Praise employees who do exceptional work.* We all want to be

appreciated, and appreciation for our efforts makes us work even harder. The praise must, however, be genuine and deserved.

12. *Be consistent.* It is impossible for an employee to do what is expected of him if his manager is not consistent in his requirements.

The above suggestions do not represent everything that managers can do to improve their personnel relations, but they can help managers to tune into their employees' needs. A manager should develop an attitude that will allow him to continue to improve in in his management abilities. The major concern of the management of any business is to generate profits and growth for the business. Bank management is faced with the same goals of profit and growth. Management must continue to understand that every employee in the bank is important and contributes to the accomplishment of the bank's goals. The major concern is to insure that the contributions made by every employee are positive ones, and that every employee is motivated to do his best.

Humanistic managers will continue to demand excellence from themselves and their employees, but they will not expect perfection. They will do everything possible to help each employee fulfill his individual potential and ambitions as long as they are consistent with the goals of the organization. The manager will always work toward the accomplishment of the goals of the organization. He also will concentrate on the goals of his employees. The employees' needs and feelings are important to him. The humanistic/participative manager knows the development of the employees of the organization will determine the success of the organization.

Increased Productivity and Employee Satisfaction

Ted R. Tompkins

The mandate for any business concern and its C.E.O. in the waning years of the 20th century will be to see that its business survives, grows, and is profitable. The achievement of these goals demands the application of techniques which traditional management as a whole has not exercised.

Business and industry leaders are in basic agreement that management's primary goal is the optimum utilization of a firm's various assets. Today's economic environment has many of our North American business concerns troubled. We see our businesses losing out or being threatened by foreign competitors, double-digit inflation, interest rates that demand restraint on capital investments, and a return on assets and/or investment unacceptable and unattractive to shareholders.

The challenge facing North American business leaders today is most formidable. They must find ways to improve their organizations' productivity in order to overcome these adversities. This lack of

94

productivity, coupled with wage increases relating to or tied directly to the inflationary rate, has been devastating to many North American concerns. Undoubtedly, most traditional leaders will undertake programs such as reduction of overhead expense, trimming budgets, and discouraging major capital expenditures for more productive equipment due to higher interest rates and marginal profits. These still remain sound management decisions but will not, in themselves, improve corporate standings.

With the advent of the present economic woes and, in some industries, a pessimistic hopelessness, North American businesses which have long range plans to remain viable enterprises *must* turn to the one option they have. This option has remained basically whole and untouched, namely capitalizing on their most important assets, their employees—an ever-changing, intangible asset that cannot be taken for granted. Disregard for this resource cannot continue. We must now put into practice the very principle we have so often given lip service to, the *people principle*.

A definite requirement for the successful operation of any business is the need for productive employees who are working effectively to accomplish goals, their own *personal goals* and the *goals of their company*. Human Resource assets (people) must now be given attention and nurtured for the benefit of all. We must adopt the belief that Human Resources (people) must be treated with dignity and consideration. People need something to believe in and to which they can contribute. Furthermore, large companies are made up of a number of individuals who need leadership and a clear understanding of company goals. We must do whatever is necessary to instill confidence in leadership. We must, if we accept this challenge, put into perspective some important points.

To gain productivity, morale must be boosted. To accomplish this, morale must emanate from the top along with good attitudes. Simply stated, enthusiasm, commitment, and a positive attitude must be promoted. Management must turn its attention to the work force and show *genuine* concern for its well-being. It must be remembered, as programs are implemented, that each person is an individual. It also must be remembered that attitudes are developed over a long period of time, so that attempts to break down the traditional adversarial roles may be met with skepticism. Expectations must be realistic when first approaching the work force. Progress must be judged accordingly.

The strategy developed must, out of necessity, be based on establishing proper lines of communication. We have to talk and get people to listen. More important, management must be prepared to listen because, ultimately, any business which is to survive has to accept the fact that it can only do so if it's allowed to by its people. This has to be accepted as the cost of corporate survival of the Eighties. We can no longer overlook or disregard the potential of people. We need to harness the powerful force of people, their minds, and their commitment. A timely quote credited to Clarence Francis, Chairman of the Board of General Foods Corporation, some forty years ago is as appropriate today as then:

> You can buy a man's time, you can buy a man's physical presence at a given place, you can even buy a measured number of skilled muscular motions per day or per hour. But you cannot buy enthusiasm.... initiative.... loyalty. You cannot buy the devotion of hearts, minds, and souls. You have to win these things.

As one gains more prominence in an organization, the ability to understand and work creatively with people-related organizational problems becomes increasingly important.

With an authoritative management style, we usually spend our valuable management time solving or attending to the basically imaginary problems of two percent of the work force, This consumes roughly ninety-eight percent of our time. Conversely, a humanistic/participative management style would permit us to utilize ninety-eight percent of our time for ninety-eight percent of our fellow employees. If one doubts that an authoritative management style is creating this kind of situation, then question officials of any union local and ask them with what percentage of their membership they are generally occupied.

A company's management style becomes apparent when one considers the organization's *attitudinal* indicators. These indicators are absenteeism and turnover ratios, safety performance, quality program results, and, lastly, the care given to the work environment starting with the work station, housekeeping, and equipment abuse. Any one of the above presents the means to attract individual attention, whether it be to create a self-stroking economy or to lash out at the system. Some employees find job satisfaction by means of performing satisfactorily within the framework of the above-mentioned programs because they can measure their performance against norms for their peer group, whereas others find immediate attention bestowed on them if their performance is less than satisfactory.

It is well known that to gain management's immediate attention one must challenge the system. But if one performs to meet or improve upon the standard one is required to meet, doing only what is expected and doing what one is getting paid to do, getting management's approval is considerably more difficult.

An illustration of the principles outlined is best presented in the story of an actual happening in a production department of a subsidiary facility of a major multinational corporation. This department consisted of forty-seven employees, twenty-four females and twenty-three males, ranging from eighteen to sixty-two years of age. Their average seniority was twelve years and their average age was thirty-one. They were represented by an international union.

This department had been managed for some time by an authoritarian individual and was experiencing less than acceptable results in the attitudinal areas outlined earlier in this chapter. The manager had tried to bring about the required results through fear motivation. He failed to realize this style would not change the employees' thinking. Moreover, its effectiveness, at best, was temporary, because when the fear subsided the people slipped back into their old habits. Of course, this style brought about adversarial relationships and unwarranted disciplinary actions in the department.

A management change took place in this department. The new manager's humanistic/participative approach to managing had already won him a reputation within the company of being "fair but firm." He believed explicitly that results were brought about through people and subsequently placed his faith in them.

Through his management skills he brought into focus immediately the problems the department was experiencing. He set up a series of meetings with the department supervisors and employees to sort out the underlying reasons for their performance. After several meetings had taken place, it became obvious his employees' attitude toward management was one of contempt. Believing that good and bad attitudes start at the top, he immediately set out in writing the items they had brought out in the meetings so as to enable him to verify their validity.

One particular complaint was that productivity, quality, and machinery upkeep was representative of poor maintenance workmanship by the assigned mechanic. In their words the mechanic was a "bailing-wire-fix-it-man" with less than adequate skills. Their claim was that anything repaired by this particular mechanic was of temporary nature only, with resultant avoidable delays occuring daily.

The members of this department worked on an incentive system with earnings relating directly to their individual output, and as such were being penalized by this mechanic's apparent lack of motivation toward his job.

The next step was to study the mechanical "down" reports, and these lent credence to the claims of the employees. To further validate these claims, the new manager not only contacted the area engineer, but he further requested that the manufacturing agent of the equipment be present at a meeting to discuss recurring problems. During this meeting it was decided that indeed a proper preventative maintenance program would minimize the down-time. Similar equipment in other companies was experiencing nowhere near the same kind of mechanical down-time: *PRECISELY WHAT THE PEOPLE IN THE DEPARTMENT HAD BEEN CLAIMING WAS A REALITY.* A proper maintenance program was absolutely necessary and would eliminate routinely experienced delays. This in turn would enhance the earning opportunity of his employees and increase both morale in the department and the employees' trust for management.

The new manager, armed with the information, discussed the situation with the maintenance manager, who, when faced with the facts, agreed to transfer the mechanic to another area of the shop and have him replaced with a more competent mechanic.

Utilizing his understanding of the needs of the people, the new manager could now improve the earning opportunities of his employees through improved maintenance and, at the same time, minimize their frustrations. They would, he suspected, respond in a positive manner and lend support to his management philosophies of gaining results through people.

In a subsequent meeting with his department personnel and supervisors, he offered improved maintenance services. He requested his department's support and, with the exception of the skeptical union stewards and some dissenters, gained a qualified agreement to commence toward this goal. Their qualification was that they trusted his motives but if he or his supervision waivered, their assistance would be withdrawn.

A preventive maintenance program was established under the direction of the newly appointed area mechanic. This, being under the manager's direction, automatically brought about accountability on his part. Needless to say, this program was most successful.

In addition to this program, the manager asked if the other employees would assist him to evaluate the remaining critical items needing attention—namely safety, quality, housekeeping, and machine abuse. It was a common consensus of the employees that this could be done best by each department employee, on a rotating basis, conducting a daily inspection tour of the department. These inspection tours started out to be some two hours in duration. The content of written reports after the tours was meager at the start, but it was meaningful. Inspection tours considered items contrary to safety procedures, housekeeping as it applied to safety and quality, and whether quality standards were being adhered to properly. It was agreed at the outset that the reports would only reflect incidents, not individual names.

As time went on it was noticed that some of the department's dissenters were either terminating their employment or were transferring to other departments. This indicated the manager was gaining the support of the majority, who now had pride in their operation and were taking care of their own.

Six months into the program, the results were astounding; and by this time the union stewards were taking turns in rotation, performing the inspections without so much as a word from the area management. The inspection tour personnel gradually took on the responsibility of posting the current data on the department's blackboard "Management by Objective Tracking Scheme." Needless to say, this department became a leader of similar departments throughout the organization. The improved maintenance program reduced down-time, improved morale, and eliminated the need for replacing or transferring dissidents.

Within two years of the commencement of this program, the

employees decreased from forty-seven to thirty-five persons through attrition—the dissidents leaving and a processing refinement eliminating four people. The processing refinement, which eliminated four people, did not bring about a single grievance from the union—which, up until this time, had been unheard of.

What phenomenon took place? Really, nothing more than an understanding of a human being's basic needs and a listening approach leading to more open dialogue and mutual trust, or at least more understanding. When lines of communication are open people are able to perceive and gain insight, which leads to mutual trust. The employees were given the opportunity to handle responsibility as well as control their own work and they became accountable. *IT BECAME A WIN-WIN SITUATION.*

The management concepts applied by this manager promoted dignity among the team members; they understood and knew what it was like to be respected and treated like capable, responsible individuals. Likewise the management now had an effective department. They no longer had the frustration of having their energies directed at watching and policing. They now had the time to attend to their managerial function of planning.

New interest was shown in the department's Management by Objectives program, which was brought about by employee involvement and which in turn brought accountability. It was interesting to note that the employees established standards for themselves which had *higher* expectations than the optimistic expectations set by their management.

Eventually, the manager of this department was transferred to another geographical location with this company in a more senior position. His replacement, although schooled in the humanistic approach, nevertheless did not approach the department head's tasks with the same vigor. This in time was interpreted by employees as a change in management philosophy, and as a result they lost their enthusiasm. On a gradual basis they withdrew their participation, and this led the department to return to mediocrity. Both parties were clearly the losers in the newly created Lose-Lose situation.

The management techniques applied in the case described above were neither original nor unknown. They had been published in numerous books, journals, and magazines over the years. Humanistic participative management style is not something you learn once and have forever; it is a continuing learning arena. It is neither a fact nor fashion, but is actually a sincere attempt to assist fellow human beings in the pursuit of their lifelong goals while achieving corporate objectives. It is best described in a Royal Bank of Canada monthly publication which said:

> The joy of leadership and the thrill of being in charge of a group of people does not consist in doing a terrific job yourself, but in spending your last ounce of energy and encouragement and guidance to see the group crack through to success.

The complexities of organizational structuring may dissuade a manager's attempts to adapt this management style. Besides, it is time-consuming and very hard, demanding work. But the rewards are corporate and personal success, which are self-fulfilling.

Modern management concepts and programs such as Quality of Work Life, Quality Circles, Positive Reinforcement, and Productivity Sharing Plans are predicated on the principles of Humanistic/ Participative Management. The principles, if applied with sincerity and without reservation, will allow a business concern to enhance its competitive position through improved utilization of its other resources. The achievement of this goal in an organization is dependent upon adoption of humanistic principles and formation of a company philosophy which has the necessary humanistic/participative content and sincerity. Any attempt to disguise a program of this nature will not only lead to failure, but will establish a distrust which will result in self-destruction.

As stated by Carl F. Frost (Cangemi and Guttschalk, 1980),

> In the exercise of leadership, there is an initial and a singular responsibility of the leader, vis-a-vis the chief executive officer, to identify and define the mandate of the organization. The word mandate is used advisedly to state the imperatives required of the organization. These are not placed upon the company as the personal desire or prerogative of the Chief Executive Officer, even though it is the Chief Executive Officer's responsibility to articulate them.

Frost then continues in reference to a corporate mandate as it refers to its Human Resources:

> Again it is not the humanity of the Chief Executive Officer that determines this mandate. It is the action of the employees who do and will insist that their employment in this organization is the best opportunity for them; otherwise they will terminate at the earliest opportunity. It is true that some employees, including executives, paint themselves into corporate corners and haven't the courage or ability to leave. Effective management recognizes, discloses, and declares the mandate to the employees at all levels that the company affords them the best employment opportunity and responsibility. In the economic vernacular, employment here offers them the best personal and professional returns on their investments of energy, education, training, expertise, life.

To accommodate the management philosophy it is necessary to initiate changes to corporate structuring. It must permit the advocates of this management style to rise to the senior positions of authority with direction of its Human Resources. Conversely, care must be taken in restructuring to accommodate the professionals required in specialty fields.

Management skepticism about change in the work place was obvious at a 1978 conference sponsored by the Work in America Institute. Many senior managers expressed the view that not only was the human factor insignificant (relative to such things as capital investment and research and development) with respect to productivity, but also that there really was no problem with productivity within manufacturing in the United States.

Have these attitudes changed significantly to bring about the necessary changes? Let's examine an excerpt from the July/August 1981 issue of *Harvard Business Review* in an article written by Robert H. Hayes entitled, "Why Japanese Factories Work." In the article a recent Japanese visiting industrialist was quoted stating:

> I get the impression that American managers spend more time worrying about the well-being and loyalty of their stockholders whom they don't know, than they do about their workers whom they do know. This is very puzzling. The Japanese manager is always asking himself how he can share the company's success with his workers.

It is obvious in North America there is much room for improvement.

REFERENCE

Frost, Carl F. in J.P. Cangemi and G.E. Guttschalk (Eds.) *Effective Management—A Humanistic Perspective*. New York: Philosophical Library, 1980.

Delegation and Participative Management

Gar Trusley

For many years I have opened my management seminars on delegation by asking the question, "What would be your course of action if you found someone working for you who was abusing or misusing company property, materials, etc.?" The answer is always the same. "We would pursue some type of disciplinary procedure—namely, counsel, reprimand, or even terminate." It is at this point I ask audiences to identify their organization's most valuable resource. Without hesitation, they invariably state "people" are their most valuable resource. The question that follows usually solicits a long pregnant pause from audience members. "What course of action would you pursue if you discovered someone in your organization abusing or misusing your most valuable resource—namely, people?"

We often direct our attention in organizations to such "white collar" crimes as theft, sabotage, spying, or even sexual harassment, but many times we fail to deal with the most subtle, but nevertheless most critical crime over the long run, that of abuse and misuse of personnel through nonexistent or ineffective delegation.

In this article we will attempt to examine the major benefits to be derived by both the manager and the organization through effective delegation. Second, we will identify the symptoms in evidence in an organization that may tell whether or not there are delegation problems. Third, we will examine the reasons why members do not or will not delegate enough and why oftentimes subordinates are reluctant to accept delegation. Finally, we will discuss the four key ingredients of effective delegation and how the manager can incorporate these concepts in his/her humanistic/participative approach to management.

Benefits of Effective Delegation

I find that many clients and seminar participants are constantly in search of the "magic formula." That is, the formula that, when applied in the work setting, will suddenly make things better. This "formularized" thinking, in my opinion, has its origin through the education process, which focuses on the systematic approach to solving problems, especially in areas such as engineering, accounting, and data processing. Managers, particularly in these areas, have been highly trained in problem analysis, and as a result, sometimes look at their people problems wearing the same glasses they use when examining technical problems. Because people are so different, a formularized approach to management would tend to muddy the waters and only further contribute to the alienation of the American worker. To many managers, though, the lack of a proven formula only serves to heighten their frustration level when it comes to dealing with people.

My feeling is that this frustration level could be considerably decreased if a manager were to use what I consider to be one of the most viable people tools at his/her disposal, namely, the effective delegation. Delegation, if carried out properly, can assist the manager in not only developing a humanistic approach to management, but also in obtaining the necessary results that every well-functioning organization needs.

A number of years ago, Dr. Frederick Herzberg stated that the four things that turned people on about work were the opportunities for growth, achievement, recognition, and responsibility. During the last ten years, I have duplicated the Herzberg experiment over 300 times in the seminar setting and have found identical results. When asked to generate a list of those things that turn them on about their work, participants (both management and non-management) invariably stated those four factors.

Let us examine how delegation can provide employees with these turn-ons and the manager with a happier, more productive work force.

Growth

Managers sometimes mistakingly feel that the only way to assist the employee in his or her growth is by sending him off to a seminar some place or by conducting in-house training. This approach certainly benefits the employee but, in my estimation, delegation done properly can often be more practical and economical. Delegation gradually increases the subordinate's responsibilities in learning more about all factors of the work, in addition to establishing greater confidence levels. I would note at this point that increased responsibility, if handled properly, should be reinforced by the manager, while increased responsibility not carried out to expectations should be corrected immediately.

Achievement

Stress and its impact on both manager and non-manager is one of the most often discussed topic areas in business circles today. Experts in this area attribute both physiological and psychological causes to stress or stress-related conditions.

It's been my observation over the years that the individual who is thwarted in his or her efforts to achieve becomes highly frustrated, anxiety ridden, and in some cases, angry with the boss, the organization, or even himself. Participants in seminars often have complained about the fact that they go home at the end of a week feeling no sense of accomplishment, but rather with the feeling they have been "spinning their wheels."

Delegation that has results clearly outlined, along with a timetable for completion, provides a track upon which the employee can run and ultimately gauge his/her performance.

Recognition

Everyone has a need to be somebody, but oftentimes the sheer size of the organization prevents the individual from gaining the recognition he or she thrives on.

Delegation, especially the kind that involves the subordinate in major issues confronting the organization—along with exposure to upper management while carrying out the designated delegation, goes a long way to filling the "recognition vacuum" that exists in so many organizations.

Responsibility

A major part of humanizing the work environment is giving the employee a "fraction of the action."

Management is oftentimes viewed by employees as "speaking with forked tongue." "They say we're all on the team here, and that we're all one big happy family, but they make all the decisions, take all the responsibility, never ask us our opinions, never give us any authority, and generally tell us what to do."

By involving the employee more in the day-to-day operation of the organization through better delegation, management clearly indicates they are willing to give the employee more responsibility, thus heightening the employees' commitment level to organization objectives.

HOW DO YOU KNOW IF YOU HAVE A DELEGATION PROBLEM?

Through my management and consulting career, I have had an opportunity to observe many types of managers. Some of these managers utilize techniques learned through extensive educational experiences, while others apply the concepts learned in the "school of hard knocks.", Each, in his own way, may accomplish the expected results. The key to achieving those results, however, regardless of the management style, is the ability of the manager to perceive accurately when there is a problem within the work environment and to take action quickly.

Inappropriate delegation, or the total lack of delegation, usually can be related to the following: excessive turnover, over-control, and constant interruptions.

Excessive Turnover

Of course, there can be many causes of excessive turnover—poor working conditions, low pay, untrained management, over-qualified personnel—just to name a few, but one reason that often is buried in the midst of an exit interview is poor delegation.

Few exiting employees want to point the finger at a boss who, in their minds, has failed to utilize what they had to offer the organization.

Employees have the need to grow and feel they are becoming more valuable to the organization. Organizations that fail to nurture that need subsequently lose some very talented employees, or worse, retain the once-talented employee who has now adopted the attitude "What's the use of complaining, it won't help anyway."

Over-Control

One of the first things we look for when consulting in an organization with "personnel problems" is the frequency and nature of its reports and meetings.

Excessive reports and meetings may indicate that the management involved may not trust the employees and their abilities to carry out certain delegated tasks; thus, the report and/or meeting serves as a vehicle with which the manager can "check" on the employee. Certainly the monitoring of the employees' progress is important, but excessive monitoring may indicate a low trust level between manager and employee.

A manager's fear of failure can be another reason for excessive reports and meetings. It is my opinion that in many organizations (the bigger, the more prevalent) *promotions are granted to those who make the fewest mistakes or the fewest major mistakes.* Managers recognize this as being "company Hoyle" and establish a system of checking that has as its goal *no mistakes.* Unfortunately, this creates a pressurized work environment that contributes little to employee or organizational growth.

Constant Interruptions

Frequently, managers in my Time Management seminars ask my advice on dealing with subordinates who are constantly interrupting them. For example, a gentleman once asked, "What would you do about getting phone calls from employees in the middle of the night?" When asked how long he had been receiving these calls, he replied, "Fifteen years." Further discussions indicated that the people working for him, when faced with a problem, had two options. One, they could try and figure out the solution to the problem themselves, or two, call the boss. Which was easiest?

This manager had been singled out by his employees as being an easy mark. Oh, he would come in and gripe about it, but he would also solve the problem.

Few managers recognize that those constant interruptions are nothing more than the subordinates placing the "monkey on the manager's back."

WHY DON'T MANAGERS DELEGATE ENOUGH— IN SOME CASES, AT ALL?

This question has been posed to thousands of my seminar participants over the years and the following reasons reflect their experiences:

They Do Not Know How

If managers would reflect back on the amount of hours they have spent in the classroom, whether it be college, trade school, technical school, high school, or even the service, they would find that the amount of hours spent on the technical side of their profession significantly outweighs that amount of time spent on learning how to be a manager. Their definition of delegation is giving something to the employee that the manager finds either too trivial or too boring. Later in the article we'll address the mechanics of effective delegation.

They Do Not Trust Their Employees

"If you want to get something done right, do it yourself," is the lament of many a workaholic manager. Because of past bad experiences with certain employees, some managers choose to burn the midnight oil rather than "getting burned again." The frequency of "getting burned" contributes heavily to the manager's ability to trust people and subsequently his/her willingness to delegate.

Inability to Take Risks

Delegation can be a risky proposition. Each time one delegates something to an employee one takes a risk. That risk is that the employee will miss the deadline, deliver inadequate information, arrive at inaccurate conclusions, etc. That risk may then be amplified by the fact that one's superior is "counting on" the information, and failure to come up with it can only reflect on one's management inability.

Managers can avoid getting burned by establishing deadlines, setting a timetable, and developing check points in order to monitor the progress of the delegation.

WHY SUBORDINATES OFTEN DO NOT ACCEPT DELEGATION (AND IF THEY DO, IT IS WITH LITTLE OR NO ENTHUSIASM)

Fear of Criticism

For many employees, delegation is a game. The game goes something like this. The boss makes the assignment (usually vague) and requests that it be completed on a certain date (usually unrealistic). The employee responds by returning the assignment two days before the stated deadline only to find that the boss has now more time to criticize the employee's efforts and ask for a rework prior to sending the project to higher authorities.

Employees learn how to deal with this particular game by purposely avoiding the early return of delegated work, thus avoiding many times the reworking of the original assignment.

They Will Change It Anyway

Reflect back at the various times you have been promoted over the years and ask this question, "Why did I receive those promotions?" You might discover a surprising answer. Oh yes, we would like to think we received those promotions because of our abilities to plan, organize, control, and lead, but let me ask this question, "When was the last time you went home on a Friday evening, and your spouse asked how your week went, and you replied, 'Great! Monday, I did a little planning. Tuesday, we worked on organization. Wednesday, we turned to controlling. And Friday, we zeroed in on leadership'?" The truth of the matter is you fought fires all week, because that is the nature of organizational life. Consequently, *the more skilled firefighters receive the promotions!*

The tendency of a crisis-type manager is to do things his way. Employees soon become frustrated because their work never seems to measure up. The manager quickly forgets that if the employee in question could do the job at the same rate or at the same level of competency as the manager, their roles would most likely be reversed.

Lack of Authority

Often employees complain that the boss may delegate certain tasks without the corresponding amounts of authority necessary to get the job done.

A variation of this problem is the manager who delegates authority to the employee but fails to communicate to other personnel that this authority has been delegated, thus virtually rendering the employee powerless.

Lack of Feedback

The boss has just requested that you assemble a task force and address a "very critical problem" that threatens the virtual existence of the department. You're to assemble your data in report form no later than the 15th of the month. You quickly assemble your team, follow through on the assignment, and forward your report as requested. One month later you have yet to hear a thing. Did they like it? Are they going to accept our recommendation? Will we be asked to do follow-up studies? Two months later you happen to be in the boss's office on another matter. You happen to notice your report at the bottom of the in-basket slightly discolored by what appears to be two-month-old coffee stains. Your attention, however, becomes diverted by the boss saying, "Harry, what we're looking for in this assignment I'm about to give you..."

The lack of feedback is a major reason for employees' indifference to delegated tasks. The "no news is good news" approach to feedback is seldom viewed by the humanistic/participative manager as a viable method of people development.

The Key Ingredients of Effective Delegation

Delegation can be viewed as a contract between the manager and the employee. This contract stipulates that the two parties agree on (1) the responsibilities of the employee, (2) the limits of authority the employee will have, (3) the results that will be achieved, and (4) the tracking system that will be employed during the course of the delegation.

Responsibilities

Before effective delegation can take place, the manager and

employee must agree to the employee's job responsibilities and priorities. Failure of this part of the contract to be in place may result in subordinates replying to a boss in the midst of delegating a task, "That's not in my job description," or, "I'm not paid to do that."

One way to determine whether or not you and your employee agree on job responsibilities is to perform the following exercise:

A. Ask the subordinate to list his/her job responsibilities by priority (on his/her own).
B. You, in turn, do the same. That is, list what *you* think the employee's job responsibilities are by priority.
C. Mutually discuss the lists to see if there are differences, and if there are, why?

Authority

Be sure that the parameters of authority being delegated are clearly defined for the employee and remember to pass those designated levels of authority to others that the delegatee may interface with during the delegation process. This will prevent organization conflict from arising.

Results

During the time that the boss and subordinate are discussing the task that is about to be delegated, particular attention should be given to the results of the delegation. Included in these results might be such items as completion date, quality of the work expected, quantity of the work expected, or even cost considerations that need to be made in performing the delegated task. This pre-delegation discussion may take only ten minutes but will, in the long run, save time spent in rework and employee frustration.

In addition, it's advisable, upon completion of the delegated work, that the manager and employee sit down together and discuss how well the delegation went in relation to expectations, as well as those things the employee learned while carrying out the assignment.

Tracking

Many times other managers have been "burned" by subordinates who fail to get the work in on time. Frequent incidents like these contribute heavily to a manager's low trust level.

Missed deadlines, improper information, inadequate results, and generally poor work can be avoided if managers would do a better job of tracking the work.

Periodic check points should be established between the delegator and delegatee during the initial discussion of the assignment. Managers must be sure that the check points are not too frequent, for this may imply that the manager does not trust the employee's ability. Thus, the contact checking.

By periodically sitting down with the employee and discussing his or her progress and/or problems in relation to the delegated task, the manager can avoid unpleasant surprises.

In Summary

1. Plan delegation as much as possible. Avoid spur of the moment assignments that may later result in confusion and inappropriate results.
2. Try to involve the delegatee as much as possible. Higher involvement may lead to higher commitment.
3. Establish deadlines. They communicate to the delegatees that the task is important.
4. Stick with deadlines. Failure to say anything to employees who miss deadlines will most certainly contribute to further such actions on their part in the future.
5. Be sure that you and the employee agree on:
   a. The employee's responsibilities.
   b. The employee's authority limits.
   c. How the delegation will be tracked and how frequently it will be tracked.
   d. The results to be accomplished.

Good delegation makes good sense. Employees who are given an opportunity to contribute to the organization through effective delegation will assist the manager in obtaining his/her results, while at the same time developing their own skills. Thus employees will be contributing to a higher self-esteem level and, in the long run, will become a much more valuable organization resource.

Quality Circles and
Participative Management—
A Colombian Experience

Luis Armando Zarruk

Our company started out in 1958 in a town called San Gil, Colombia, South America. San Gil is located in the state of Santander. The company began producing natural fiber sacks and, at present, with its other two plants in the city of Bucaramanga, is producing sacks, cords, and plastic ropes which are sold all over Colombia. We also export them to other Latin American countries such as Panama, Venezuela, and Peru. In the three plants currently there are more than 500 hourly and salaried employees.

The brand of unionism in the state of Santander has been one of the strongest and most belligerent in Colombia. Our company was known as the one with the most labor conflicts in the region because of the numerous strikes we experienced between 1974 and 1980. The last strike, which occurred four years ago, lasted two and a half months and caused serious financial problems for the company.

The Beginning

In 1979 there were some major changes in the company. Among these changes were the positions of President, Financial Vice-President, Director of Industrial Relations, and other important administrative personnel. After the strike of 1980, the company began to evaluate its organization climate and management practices with regard to communication, employee relations, work systems, and so forth.

The result of this evaluation clearly demonstrated the necessity for the company to develop a new general policy of personnel administration. As a result, a large-scale program was initiated that culminated in a change in personnel policies and labor relations practices in the company.

An important part of the new program was the introduction of Quality Circles, renamed by us Circles of Participation. We believed that the new name would develop a higher sense of work identification in the various work groups. The introduction of Quality Circles did not originate as an isolated action, but was part of a change process precipitated from inside the company. Interestingly, once Quality Circles became a reality, they were accepted as a new responsibility for the managers.

The Motivation

At the same time that top management was surveying the labor situation we were experiencing in early 1981, we began a process to encourage the adoption of the Quality Circle program. Each manager supported the program and became responsible for it in his area.

In top management meetings, the extraordinary significance of the program for that difficult and stressful time was analyzed. Out of the meetings came the highest commitment to the program. We were all motivated by the belief that a change in personnel relations would be most beneficial to the company at that moment.

The motivation of personnel and the diffusion of the program were achieved in part through the company's bulletin. However, the direct and personal information that employees received from the administration regarding the creation of the Quality Circles program proved to be most effective. After top management showed its support for the program and the people knew that it was not an isolated action from the Department of Industrial Relations, registration was opened to participants, and the required steps were followed to put the circles into operation. These included the training of leaders and members, the study of diagrams of cause and effect, courses about dynamics of groups, the improvement of communication skills and skills of decision making, and so forth.

The Program

All employees of the company were informed about the philosophy, growth, and nature of the circles through poster boards, the company's bulletin, and, as we mentioned before, direct lectures to personnel.

A main requirement of the circles is voluntary participation; 110 hourly and salaried employees from the three plants expressed their wish to participate by registering.

We decided to start with two circles for production workers in the factories where there were the largest numbers of volunteers. The large number of volunteers offered the most hope for these sections.

Next, two groups were formed at the administration level; these groups were not exactly homogeneous in regard to their positions, but they had a common goal. In one way or another their functions would join together because they shared common problems.

While the program was in progress and expectations were being realized, we were pleased by the request from a group of technicians— mechanics, electricians, production analysts, and methods and time analysts—to form a circle. The group received approval to be established as a circle and is one of the most productive circles we have functioning.

The program's management is a coordinated committee made up of administrators representing the areas of Industrial Relations, Finance, Production, and Sales. The Manager of Industrial Relations is in charge of the program coordination. He organizes the work of the leaders and the members of the circle, and he also has the support of a facilitator.

There are fifty-nine participants in the program:

six members of the coordinating committee,
one coordinator,
one facilitator,
five leaders, and
forty-six members of circles.

There are five active circles now. Our goal is to have five more circles next year. If the goal is realized, twenty percent of the personnel would be part of the program.

The Union

The union did not support or have a positive attitude toward the program during the first months. But, when it became clear that the program of quality circles meant an open administration ready to listen to the problems of the people, and that the communications were resulting in a more dynamic and agile administration, the union's attitude changed. It did not attack the circles as it had at the beginning of the program.

The union understood that the new situation in personnel relations was the sincere result of the administration's having a more healthy and less conflictive organization.

New Policies and New Things

In addition to the forming of Quality Circles, changes have occurred in the politics of selection, promotion, and training of personnel.

The following have been established also:

Happy Birthday Cards: Each of the employees is congratulated by the president or by one of the managers of the company. This is an opportunity for a casual talk with the employee about his work.

Informal Meetings: The meetings, directed by the president and the manager of the plant, are with four or five hourly employees once every fifteen or twenty days. There is no specific topic, just an informal and spontaneous conversation.

Bulletin Boards: We post news referring to production, finance, sales, and information concerning the employees and the good functioning of the company.

Newsletters: At the moment a bulletin is published monthly with information about social events, sports, the participation circles, and so forth.

Surveys: Every year a survey is conducted of about fifteen percent of the company's personnel. The questions asked relate to the following:
    their more important problems,
    how they think the company is working, and
    what worries them the most about the company, markets, and
        so forth.

The answers to the survey are taken into consideration in the development of new programs.

Lunch Programs

Each week a top management executive has lunch with a group of six or seven hourly employees. The informal lunch in a local restaurant offers a good opportunity for the president and managers to get to know the personnel, their anxieties toward the company, their families, and so forth.

These are some of the programs that are in progress in our company. All the programs are simple; we have read about them in administration books many times, but only when we practice them do we know their beneficial effects on keeping organizations healthy. Through simple things like these, the people develop feelings of security, appreciation, respect, and acceptance.

Quality Circles and Participative Management

The three years of experience with the program of Quality Circles have shown us the way toward a participative administration. The members and leaders of the circles have developed their abilities to:

interact in groups,
listen and be listened to,
conduct meetings, and
state solutions to the managers in order to make proper decisions.

The circles of managers' secretaries have solved more than fifty problems this year! The biggest satisfaction I have had since I began working with organizations came the day that the circle formed by secretaries presented to the president the solution to the company's filing system problem.

Through their study of the problem, the members of the circle learned about:

the legal requirements, Colombian Laws, and the filing of microfilm;
the three companies with the best filing systems in the city (companies they visited);
the basic financial methods to evaluate the economic proposals of the experts in filing systems; and
administering the economy of the company.

When the presentation ended, one of the secretaries came to me and said: "The most interesting experience for me hasn't been to learn about the filing system, but the discovery of my potential as a human being.... I have learned to have success."

At the moment, the circles are developing activities relating to the improvement of communication and changes in processes in production and reduction of waste.

Right now, we have not just ten or fifteen people identifying the company's problems. We have more than seventy people thinking about problems that before were considered the exclusive responsibility of the company. In the future we'll have more people doing this.

The participation that is solving the company's problems is reaching all levels of the organization. However, the decisions made and their consequences are the responsibility of the managers.

The results of Quality Circles and the other programs which I mentioned have a high value in terms of improvement in the organization, and in the future these will be among the strengths of the company.

If we want to view the results in economic terms, we can do that too. In the last three years the company has not invested in the development of its new personnel programs an amount more than the cost of one of the strikes of previous years. To say the least, Quality Circles are proving to be a most successful experience in our company.

Participatory Management in Organizations of Higher Education

Casimir J. Kowalski
and
J. Richard Bryson

The principal responsibility of the college administration is to bring about institutional unity among individuals with clashing intellectual ideas. The college administrator must be, first of all, an educated individual with a fundamental understanding of the broad divisions of knowledge; secondly, an individual who has certain technical, social and leadership skills in order to guide college intellectuals on the one hand and community citizens on the other (Gibson, 1969).

Critics of higher education have charged that many colleges and universities are among the worst managed institutions in the United States. It has been argued that most colleges and universities today are run by strangers to their faculties. Hospitals and some state and city administrations may be as bad. However, no business or industry except perhaps Penn Central, according to many critics, can possibly be managed as poorly as the American college. One reason for this poor management is that universities have studied everything from government to Persian mirrors, but few have ever studied deeply their own administration practices.

The present crisis in higher education calls for leadership. But many leaders are not leading; they are consulting, pleading, temporizing, martyrizing, trotting, putting out fires, and avoiding or taking the heat (and spending too much energy doing both). They have sweaty palms, and they are scared. One reason is that many of them do not appear to understand what leadership is all about. Like Auden's Captain, they are studying navigation while the ship is sinking. In higher education we need leaders at the top, not just managers. There is an important difference between the two. Managers tend to organize, control and direct an organization's efforts. They often get bogged down with paper, and managers are basically active. Leaders, on the other hand, become less involved in these kinds of activities and become more concerned with the direction in which the organization is heading, how it is going to get there—including the resources necessary to get there—as well as other creative endeavors (Bennis, 1976).

Many institutions are very well managed but very poorly led. The leader must create for his institution clear cut, measurable goals based on advice from all elements of the academic community (Bennis, 1976). Somewhere between these *extremes* of order, trust and stability, versus disorder, distrust and uncertainty, there is an optimal point where order prevails, and flexibility and openness still exist. Policies are made on the basis of information from appropriate sources within the organization. Decisions are reached on the basis of cooperation among many informed individuals. *The philosophy of management is one in which individuals are important.* Indeed, individuals are viewed as human resources, as vital to the organization as the natural and technical resources. The atmosphere is one of trust, cooperation, respect, and confidence. It is one of order and direction, but always open to suggestions and improvement. The individual finds recognition in doing a good job, feels responsible for his actions and has a sense of belonging. He is proud to be identified as a member of the department or office, and sees his future, to some extent, as being dependent upon the success of the organization. The growth of members within the organization is in keeping with the purpose of the organization (House, 1974).

Participatory Management In The Decision-Making Process

In any organization, decisions need to be made, and the best way to make them is to gather all the facts. The decision-making process is an art as well as a science. There are three distinct ways in which decisions may be reached in an organization: authoritarian, democratic, and complete freedom—absence of control and direction (Schien, 1970).

Perhaps one of the most dominant features of any organization is its decision-making process. Decisions differ in terms of content, time perspectives, and in the number and type of individuals who make them. Indeed, the *process* of decision making can have as much influence over the relationship between an individual and the organization as the *content* of the decision itself. The decision-making process has impact not only upon the direction in which the organization moves, but also upon the professional and psychological growth of its members (House, 1974).

Despite the widespread support for the participatory leadership approach, relatively few mechanisms have been found in securing such participation into an operational reality. According to Pollay, Taylor and Thompson (1976), the following benefits could potentially be derived from allowing faculty/staff participation in the decision-making process:

1. Increased supervisor effectiveness
2. Faculty satisfaction
3. Decreased student alienation
4. Improved student achievement
5. Ability to reduce organization complexity by synthesizing the contributions of individuals with various organizational perspectives

6. Acceptance of decisions by all parties to the decision
7. Democratizing a rapidly hierarchical organization and providing all levels of employees with some element of control over their own fates, especially when participation is used to establish goals
8. Rebuilding of academic communities within the university structure

Decision-Making Process

Katz and Kahn (1966) reported that organizations in which influential acts are widely shared are generally more effective. First, people have a greater feeling of commitment to decisions in which they have participated. Second, wide distribution of the leadership function is likely to improve the quality of decisions. Schien (1970) has written that group participation, within an environment of trust, can work as quickly and effectively as authoritarian decision making. In the absence of mutual trust and confidence, however, group processes are likely to be slower and less efficient than an individual decision maker.

Tannenbaum (1966) also reported that systems of control which give the individual more say about his work in the organization can be conducive to efficiency. *The participative approach is more rewarding psychologically to members of the organization.*

Educational theorists such as Corson (1973) and Millett (1962) have advocated participation of all segments of the college community in the decision-making process. Every person should be given the opportunity to contribute to the decisions relating to the functions he/she performs. Mistakes are going to be made, but hopefully growth will take place from experiencing the consequences of a wrong decision as well as experiencing the consequences of a good one.

Likert (1961) stated that organizations must provide more clear cut economic rewards for behavior which helps the organization achieve its objectives. He was quick to add, however, that in addition to the effective use of economic needs, managers must strive to use other noneconomic motivators such as praise and participation.

A review of the literature Cangemi and Guttschalk (1980), Corson

(1973), Duyrea (1973), Gibson (1969), Katz and Kahn (1966), Likert (1961), Lumley (1979), Maslow (1968), Mayo (1971), Millett (1962), Pollay, et al. (1976), Schien (1970) and Tannenbaum (1966) strongly supports implementation of a *participative management* approach to leadership, away from the rigid hierarchical organization of institutions of higher education. The authors of this article define *participatory management as having a central theme of subordinate influence in decision making.* In other words, faculty/staff are *involved* in making decisions that affect them. They share authority with their top administrators.

Participatory Management In Higher Education

A humanistic, participatory philosophy of management in higher education has been the theme at many institutions of higher education today. Evidence suggests that this kind of environment allows individuals to reach their maximum potential. As previously stated, the most important contribution a president and his administrative staff can give to the institution is pulling all the forces of the institution together. According to Gibson (1969), who himself was a college president, the management of colleges and universities should be a participative enterprise among administrators, professors and students.

Various efforts have been undertaken at some colleges and universities to pull together the central forces within the institution essentially through humanistic management (Theory Y). This has been accomplished by the steady nurturing of Theory Y management behavior on the part of the president of the institution and his administrators. This basic managerial philosophy reflects a belief in the potential of people to be able to utilize most of their capabilities if given the opportunity to do so (McGregor, 1960).

In the mid-seventies, the faculty and staff of various institutions of higher learning, aware of past experience in institutions which failed to consider adequately the individual and his/her needs in the organizational context, resolved not to squander their resources in similar manner. They began to develop a management system which recognized the worth and dignity of each individual. They recognized the human potential in their organizations as a vital contributing element and set about to create institutions which would acknowledge its human resources as being at least as important as their financial and physical resources. They agreed on two basic beliefs:

1. A single individual cannot possess consummate expertise and knowledge to arbitrarily determine the direction a growing institution is to develop or unilaterally make the decision to get it there.
2. A single individual cannot be held accountable for assumed or assigned responsibilities if not granted the commensurate authority.

In short, the faculty and staff agreed that if their institutions were to succeed, they had to decide together where they were going, then utilize *all* available resources to get them there. To do less would limit individual and institutional growth opportunities and problem solving capabilities. The professional literature referred to such an approach to management as "humanistic," "cooperative," "shared authority," "democratic decision making," etc. The label used today is *participatory management*.

An important factor in this philosophy and process is the role and function at the Director/Department level; the amount of authority commensurate with the responsibility. The role of Department Director (chairperson) is much more responsible than at most institutions. This is evidenced by the responsibility and authority assigned to budget development and expenditure, hiring and supervision of faculty, evaluation process of faculty, decisions in merit allocations at the department level, responsibility for curriculum, and numerous other functions.

Implementing Participatory Management

Participatory management recognizes the need to develop a system of management that:

1. Provides occasion to identify college opportunities, concerns, and problems;
2. Provides a vehicle to identify and implement activities to take

advantage of the opportunities and / or remedy the problems for which specific individuals would be held accountable;
3. Provides assurance that the rights and interests of the institution, groups, and individual would be considered in any decision.

Probably the best way to identify opportunities and concerns in an institution of higher learning is to ask those most knowledgeable about them, and most affected by the decisions being made to accommodate them: board members, faculty, staff, students and alumni. One institution used the Individual, Institutional, Organizational Unit (HOU) Survey technique. Modeled after the Delphian Nominal Group Techniques, it permitted *all* college constituencies an opportunity not only to identify meaningful suggestions and concerns but also to prioritize each according to their importance to the individual and the future direction of the organization. While such a technique permitted better utility of its human resources, it likewise provided a forum in which to compare ideas. People were heard. People saw many of their suggestions, whether significant or insignificant, become implemented. A list of concerns and problems was identified and later these concerns became objectives. One of the easiest ways participatory management can be destroyed is for people to *not* observe any follow-up from surveys in which they participated. Such practices lead people to believe their ideas fell on deaf ears; they also generate the feeling they merely took part in an administrative exercise.

It is incumbent upon the institution of higher education to develop a method to incorporate specific suggestions and concerns obtained into college objectives, stating what needs are to be accomplished and who is accountable for accomplishing them. In other words, a system of managing an institution is needed which focuses on planning and controlling for specific results while clearly stating what is accomplished and by whom. One such system was the Management By Objectives (MBO) concept. This concept stresses a continual process whereby top administrators, department heads, faculty and staff periodically identify institutional goals and objectives, define each group's / individual's major areas of responsibility in terms of expected results, and use these agreed-upon objectives as guides for operating and assessing each department's contribution in support of the mission of the institution.

In one particular college, the objectives and activities were organized into an institutional plan and submitted to the College Committee for review. The College Committee was composed of representatives of the four constituencies (faculty, administration, clerical staff and students) of the college, empowered to sit in formal session to review institutional policy and operation and to recommend institutional changes, accommodate resolution of problems, and to generate means and direction for institutional development. The responsibilities include reviewing policies recommended for adoption by the college constituencies and recommending action for increasing effective and efficient functioning of the college in such areas as institutional purposes and goals, institutional planning and budget analysis, institutional organization/operational systems, institutional communications and intra-institutional and inter-institutional cooperation. After revision and final approval by the College Committee, the college plan, with its objectives and activities, was submitted to the president for his review, revision, and approval. It was then submitted to the Board of Trustees for the same process.

The participatory management philosophy is alive and well at numerous institutions of higher education. Results, both objective and subjective, are in evidence at many colleges and universities and lend validity to the perception that participatory management can, and does, work if properly nurtured by top administrators in a collegial environment. Below are examples of the results obtained through participatory management at one college committed to the participatory management process.

Objective Results

— College accreditation by North Central Association
— Re-accreditation of various programs
— Steady growth in enrollment
— Greater community acceptance and support
— Cooperative and positive efforts in response to state-mandated budget cut backs
— Voluntary participation (95%) in the college-wide IIOU survey

Subjective Results

— Employee stability and very low turnover
— No efforts by faculty to become unionized
— Greater eagerness by individuals to participate on college committees
— Comments by visitors and accreditation team that people seem to enjoy coming to work
— Visitors describe an existence of a positive and healthy atmosphere
— Positive feedback expressed by part-time faculty about working at the college
— Enhanced departmental cohesion
— Increased faculty pride and identification with the institution

In conclusion, the experiences reported in several institutions of higher education through the utilization of humanistic management suggest that many more such institutions would be able to harness the enormous power contained within them if they adopted a participative, humanistic management philosophy. The authors of this article highly recommend humanistic management in institutions of higher education as a viable management style for the 1980's and 1990's. It will result in a wholesome, positive, growth-oriented work environment. It will likewise lead to union avoidance.

REFERENCES

Bennis, W. *The Unconscious Conspiracy—Why Leaders Can't Lead*. New York: AMACOM Division of American Management Association, 1976.

Cangemi, J.P. & G.E. Guttschalk. *Effective Management—A Humanistic Perspective*. New York, New York: Philosophical Library, 1980.

Corson, J.J. "Perspective On The University Compared With Other Institutions." In James A. Perkins, *The University As An Organization*. New York: McGraw-Hill Book Co., 1973.

Duryea, E.D. "Evolution of University Organizations." In James A. Perkins, *The University As An Organization*. New York, McGraw-Hill Book Co., 1973.

Gibson, R.C. *The Challenge of Leadership In Higher Education*. Dubuque, Iowa: Wm. C. Brown Co. Publishers, 1969.

House, S.C. *Application of Selected Principles of Organization Theory To Institutions of Higher Education*. Bloomington, Indiana: Dissertation, Indiana University, August 1974.

Katz, D. & R.L. Kahn. *The Social Psychology of Organizations*. New York: John Wiley and Sons, Inc., 1966.

Kowalski, C.J., & J.P. Cangemi. "Higher Education: Its Development and Impact—A Brief Review of the Literature." *College Student Journal Monograph*, Feb./March 1974, *8*.

Likert, Rensis. *New Patterns of Management*. New York: McGraw-Hill Book Co., 1961.

Lumley, D.D. "Participation in Educational Design Making." *Educational Horizons*, Spring 1979, 57, 123-125.

Maslow, A.H. *Eupsychian Management*. Homewood, Illinois: R.D. Irwin Co., 1968.

Mayo, E. "Hawthorne And The Western Electric Company." In D.S. Pugh, *Organizational Theory: Selected Readings*. Baltimore, Maryland: Penguin Books, Inc., 1971.

McGregor, D. *The Human Side of Enterprise*. New York: McGraw-Hill Book Co., 1960.

Millett, J.D. *The Academic Community*. New York: McGraw-Hill Book Co., 1962.

Pollay, R.W., R.N. Taylor, & M. Thompson. "Model for Horizontal Power Sharing and Participation in University Decision Making." *The Journal of Higher Education*, March/April 1976, *47, (2)*, 141-152.

Schien, E.H. *Organizational Psychology*. Englewood Cliffs, New Jersey: Prentice-Hall, 1970.

Tannenbaum, A.S. *Social Psychology of the Work Organization*. Belmont, California: Wadsworth Publishing Co., Inc., 1966.

Building a More Positive Attitude Toward the Company: The Annual Employee Earnings and Benefits Letter

Jeffrey C. Claypool
Joseph P. Cangemi

Employee benefits are, of course, very common in the business world today. It is rare to find an employer who does not have some kind of benefit plan for such areas as pension and life, accident and medical insurance. Employee benefit programs accumulate and disburse large sums of money to employees, and their costs have risen faster than those of any other compensation component. According to the U.S. Chamber of Commerce, in September 1976, benefit costs per employee rose by 387% during the period from 1955 to 1975. The average worker's base annual income during the same period increased 92%, the Consumer Price Index 98.6%, and corporate taxes nearly 100%, according to the U.S. Government Council of Economic Advisors. Presently, benefit costs range from about 19% to over 60% of total compensation expenses. Contrary to the belief of those who consider benefits a low priority item, benefit costs for the average employer could rise to approximately 68% of total compensation by 1985, based on the cost trend of the past two decades (Hanna, 1975).

Fringe benefits are extremely important in attracting and maintaining an adequate employment level and in building more positive employee attitudes toward the company. With skillful planning, the fringe benefit package becomes an indispensable component of a successful business. Yet, there is ample research to demonstrate that these objectives are not being attained, largely because of poor communication. Thus, a fringe benefit plan requires constant administrative attention.

Poor Employee Recall

Many employees give little thought to the question of how much is spent on their behalf by their company. Studies have demonstrated that, when questioned, some employees cannot recall even 15% of the benefits they receive or to which they are entitled (Holley and Engram, 1973).

Obviously, management *must* spend a certain amount of time informing employees of the magnitude of these payments. In fact, failure to provide employees with this information can negatively influence their attitudes toward the employer.

On the other hand, making employees aware of what their company does for them—those "extras" which are not evident in their paychecks—should have a favorable effect on most individuals. Once the benefit programs and their monetary values are explained, management should then emphasize the need for employees to help increase the company's competitive position, so that survival and growth can continue. This knowledge will not necessarily motivate them to be more productive per se. However, it will help create a better employee attitude and will also assist in developing a good image of the organization within the community. And these improvements can result in intangible future savings.

A SAMPLE EMPLOYEE EARNINGS AND BENEFITS LETTER

COMPANY NAME
ADDRESS

DATE

Employee's Name
Address

Dear . . . .

Enclosed are your W-2 forms showing the amount of taxable income that you received from during 1980. Listed below in Section A are your gross wages and a cost breakdown of various fringe benefit programs that you enjoy. In addition to the money you received as wages, the company paid benefits for you which are not included in your W-2 statement. These are fringe benefits that are sometimes overlooked. In an easy-to-read form, here's what . . . . paid to you in 1980:

Section A—Paid to You in Your W-2 Earnings

Cost-of-Living Allowance _____
Shift Premium _____
Suggestion Award(s) _____
Service Award(s) _____
Vacation Pay _____
Holiday Pay _____
Funeral Pay _____
Jury-Duty Pay _____
Military Pay _____
Accident & Sickness Benefits _____
Regular Earnings _____
Overtime Earnings _____
Allowances _____

GROSS WAGES _____

Section B—Paid for You and Not Included in Your W-2 Earnings:

Company Contribution to Stock Purchase & Savings Plan _____
Company Contribution to Pension Plan _____
Company Cost of Your Hospitalization Payments _____
Company Cost of Your Life & Accidental Death Insurance _____
Company Cost for Social Security Tax on Your Wages _____
Company Cost of the Premium for Your Workers Compensation _____
Company Cost for the Tax on Your Wages for Unemployment
    Compensation _____
Company Cost for Tuition Refund _____
Company Cost for Safety Glasses _____

TOTAL COST OF BENEFITS NOT INCLUDED
    IN W-2 EARNINGS _____

TOTAL _____ PAID
    FOR YOUR SERVICES IN 1980 _____

You have earned the amount on the bottom line, but we want to give you a clearer idea of the total cost of your services to the company, and the protection and benefits that are being purchased for you and your family.

Sincerely,

Personnel Manager

Tailoring the Tool

The "Employee Earnings and Benefits Letter" is an example of a practical benefit communication tool. Such a letter could be distributed to each employee every January. Data would first be collected and the letter printed by the data processing department. The personalized letter would then be sent to each employee, either prior to or at the same time as the W-2 form. This letter would not only explain to the employees the cost of various fringe benefits, but would also list all of the benefits on one sheet, so that everyone could quickly review all the benefits to which he or she was entitled.

Section A of the letter should list the employee's gross wages and a cost breakdown of the various fringe benefits, such as cost-of-living allowance; shift premium; suggestion awards; service awards; payment for holidays, funerals, jury duty, military training and vacations; accident and sickness benefits; regular earnings; overtime earnings; and allowances. The item in Section A should then be totaled and the gross wages earned by the employee listed for his or her review.

Other fringes that might also be itemized in Section A are listed below:

1) Amount of paid time-off to conduct charity drives or support for community activities and organizations,
2) Amount of paid time-off because of illness in the family or to keep medical and dental appointments,
3) Coffee or smoking breaks,
4) Lunch break,
5) Portal-to-portal pay,
6) Cash bonus,
7) Wash-up time,
8) Scholarships for employees' children,
9) Social and recreational programs,
10) Parking facilities,
11) Work clothes,
12) Food service,
13) Medical facilities,
14) Employee communications and newspaper,

15) Incentive pay,
16) Matching donations to colleges and universities,
17) Relocation expenses,
18) Orientation and training,
19) Banking services,
20) Company automobile,
21) Club membership,
22) Stock bonus.

In addition to the money that employees receive as wages, it is advisable to highlight the benefits paid for them that are not included in the W-2 statements. Examples of these benefits are listed in Section B of the letter.

A Translation of Values

Considering the investment that companies make in establishing and improving fringe benefits with the expectation that they will promote positive employee behavior, it appears that many of these same companies do very little to translate the benefits into a monetary value dimension that is easily understood and appreciated by most employees. The word "security," which is usually synonymous with such benefits, has several different meanings to different people. However, a monetary value can be easily understood and translated into security by all employees, who will then better appreciate the magnitude of what the company is doing for them.

REFERENCES

Hanna, John B. *"Can the Challenge of Escalating Benefit Costs Be Met?" The Personnel Administrator*, March-April 1973.
Holley, William H., Jr. and Earl Engram, II. "Communicating Fringe Benefits." *The Personnel Administrator*, March-April 1973.

Ethical Behavior and Mental Health in Organizations

Joseph P. Cangemi

In attempting to review the topic of ethical behavior in a number of management and organizational psychology texts, this writer was surprised at the lack of information available on the subject. It almost appeared as though the subject was deliberately avoided. It certainly proved to be an area not too many writers delved into as they ventured their way into writing about managing people, managing organizations, and organizational behavior in general.

Ethics is defined as principles of conduct governing an individual or a group. Ethics often refers to a code of behavior. This code is not necessarily written; it is usually unwritten in organizations. Often, the ethical code governing organization behavior can be observed in the behavior of the leaders of the organization.

How is ethical behavior established? How is an ethical code determined? How does an organization decide what its ethical posture will be? According to Atchison and Hill (1978),

> Whether a given set of activities, interactions, and decisions is seen as ethical depends on the values of the people who are asking the question.

This now leads to the area of mental hygiene and emotional maturity. According to Vaughan (1962), individuals who are emotionally mature also usually enjoy a high degree of mental health. Vaughan suggests the two concepts are very much interrelated. In reviewing additional literature on mental health, Rogers (1980), Maslow (1970), Goble (1972), and Cangemi (1977) link ethical behavior to mental hygiene. In general, they observe that the most ethical conduct, the most ethical behavior, appears to be a central core of the overall behavior pattern of the most healthy individuals. In other words, *the most ethical behavior generally comes from the most mature, mentally healthy people.*

According to Sutich (1949), the most mature people, the most mentally healthy individuals, move into even superior behavior (which Maslow termed self-actualizing behavior) and demonstrate numerous positive behaviors in a rather consistent manner. Among these behaviors are superior judgment and wisdom, as well as a superior value system. This value system includes a solid core of ethical standards that includes caring about others, concern for others, compassion for others, fair play with others, and honesty in dealing with others. These mature people strive to behave in ways, to do things in ways, which they can be proud of and that are in consonance with their internalized, humane value system. They *choose* to behave this way because they have *empathy*; that is, they can feel the effects of their values, ethical standards, and resultant behavior on others who are affected by them.

If institutions of education, particularly higher education, are to address the topic of developing ethical conduct in their graduates, it seems to make some sense that they must first concentrate on helping individuals develop into mature personalities, into emotionally mature human beings.

What are these people like? Some observed and validated characteristics of the most mature people are the following. They have a good self-image, they like themselves and have a high degree of respect for themselves. This then frees them to like and to respect genuinely others. According to Maltz (1960),

> The person who feels that people are not very important, cannot have very much deep-down self-respect and self-regard—for he himself is

"people" and with what judgment he considers others, he himself is unwittingly judged in his own mind.

They are tolerant of others, can accept ideas from others, can admit mistakes, have a high degree of self-confidence, have less need for approval from others—but can easily give approval to others, learn from mistakes, are quite interested in others and have good facility for understanding their motives, have humility, have a positive attitude and are relaxed and patient, have a high degree of self-discipline, and are responsible. They have a high degree of awareness, both of themselves and their environment, and consequently are little afraid of the unknown. They do not seek safety usually; they seek challenge. As a result, they see things as they really are and are not very defensive. In short, these are people who have developed themselves well, and with this development has come the growth of a set of values solidly buttressed by a genuine concern for the rights and feelings of others. Consonant with this value system is a positive code of conduct (ethics) governing their behavior both toward themselves and others that can be labeled *considerate*, *respectful*, *honest*, and *fair*.

In sum, the study of ethical behavior seems, to this writer, incomplete without taking into consideration the emotional maturity of those making the decisions. It appears that, on a more consistent basis, the most ethical conduct—the healthiest code of behavior— will be observed in the most mature, the most mentally healthy individuals. The implication for organizations of higher education is that serious efforts and inroads must be made at helping individuals, while they are still students, move along a path of healthy growth and development so that by the time they are graduates they will be firmly entrenched in this direction and process and will continue developing into the most mature adults and citizens.

The implications for business, industrial, and other types of organizations are lucid. When searching for individuals to fill key leadership roles they must make every effort to select *only the most mentally healthy candidates* if their organizations are to be permeated by a healthy code of ethics. Certainly, participative management, the focus of this book, as a leadership style, has little hope of being utilized in an organization headed by leaders who do not possess a healthy code of ethics—or who do not demonstrate healthy behavior themselves. Indeed, those organizations that pay little attention to the mental-hygiene status of their leaders can expect to find a code of ethics emanating from the top that, in the long run, will prove to be disastrous for them.

REFERENCES

Atchison, T.J. and W.W. Hill. *Management Today*. New York: Harcourt, Brace, Jovanovich, 1978.

Cangemi, J.P. *Higher Education and the Development of Self-Actualizing Personalities*. New York: Philosophical Library, 1977.

Goble, F. *Excellence in Leadership*. New York: American Management Association, 1972.

Maltz, M. *Psycho-Cybernetics*. Hollywood, California: Wilshire Publishing Company, 1960.

Maslow, A. *Motivation and Personality*. New York: Harper and Row, 1970, Second Edition.

Rogers, C. *A Way of Being*. New York: Harper and Row, 1980.

Sutich, A. "The Growth-Experience and the Growth-Centered Attitude." *Journal of Psychology*, 1949, *28*, 293-301.

Vaughan, W. *Personal and Social Adjustment*. New York: Odyssey Press, 1962.

Ethics, Values, and Productivity

Charles L. Eison, James R. Craig and Charles M. Ray

Introduction

Work can be conceptualized as a sociotechnical system that requires both the necessary technology (e.g., tools) and the appropriate social structure to relate the people to the technology and individuals to one another (Cummings and Molloy, 1977). Technology without the structure results in low levels of task performance and little, if any, productive work being accomplished. Such a conceptualization of work indicates that the task of management becomes one of organizing the interaction of the requisite technology and the social structure so that productivity is maximized. Many management strategies have been proposed for that purpose and have operated with varying degrees of success. One such review of those strategies has been reported (Eison and Craig, 1982) and suggests that the strategies can be categorized into one of four basic approaches: job and reward manipulation strategies, interpersonal relationship manipulation strategies, system-wide strategies, and data collection and feedback strategies (see Table 1). The important point is not that the management strategies can be categorized, but rather that there has been considerable effort expended in organizing interaction systems to relate people to technology so that work may be accomplished. It is our contention that some of these management procedures are more successful than others in particular situations because the strategies are consistent with the value held by both managers and employees. And, it is these values that are reflected in codes of ethical conduct.

Management Ethics

Some would argue that ethics are not a proper concern of management—especially in business. In part, this is because the term ethics brings to mind moralistic rules of conduct that are commonly designated to the legitimate realm of such social institutions as churches and schools. This view is too narrow, however.

In general, ethics refer to the kind of behavior that enables people to live and work together in a free society (Stone, 1980). Societies have long legislated codes of ethics to attempt to insure members of a society are ethical in their conduct (i.e., affirmative action or equal employment opportunity). In addition, codes of ethics have been adopted by many professions. In each instance, the major thrust has been to develop a standard set of procedures each individual can understand and use in guiding his or her behavior. Such codes of conduct—rules of the game if you will—comprise the *stated values* or *ethics* of a group or an individual and may or may not be reflected in the behavior of the person—the *ethics (values)-in-use*.

Ethics and Productivity

Productivity is a major concern in the United States today. Many solutions have been offered to business leaders as strategies that can be implemented to increase productivity—flex-time, work life improvement, and management by objectives are but a few of the alternatives suggested (refer to Table 1). However, most of these strategies have been directed toward single sets of outcome objectives and have failed to address system-wide problems of interfacing pro-

Table 1. Types of Change Strategies Instituted
to Increase Worker Productivity.

Description	Behavioral Outcomes in Conjunction with Increased Productivity
1. Job and Reward Manipulation Strategies (e.g., profit sharing, job re-arrangement, reward scheduling, Scanlon Plan, flex-time, job enrichment, sales awards, and piece rates)	a. Improved morale b. Increased group participation c. Reduced worker frustration
2. Interpersonal Relationship Manipulation Strategies (e.g., team building, T-groups, quality circles, matrix structures, stress management, and motivational training)	a. Reduced worker frustration b. Increased job satisfaction c. Improved interpersonal competence
3. System-Wide Strategies (e.g., formal theory applications, human resource development programs, quality of worklife programs, Theory Z, Theory Y, process consultation, and organizational development)	a. Increased pride in being a member of the organization b. Improved leadership opportunities c. Increased job satisfaction
4. Data Collection and Feedback strategies (e.g., systems analysis, management by objectives, statistical quality control systems, program evaluation, and management information systems)	a. Increased management efficiency b. Reduced worker waste c. Legitimatized reward system

duction technology and the social structure of the work place. This has happened primarily because there has been a discrepancy between management's stated ethics (values) and their ethics (values)-in-use.

Management's objective has been to maximize profit through maximizing productivity and minimizing cost. Traditionally, profits have been only begrudgingly shared with employees and have been viewed as occurring as the result of the efforts of management—not workers. Thus, while the stated ethics (values) of management in the Western world are generally democratic, egalitarian in nature (Ray and Eison, 1983), the manager's ethics (values)-in-use often reflect decidedly different values. The ethics (values)-in-use have often dictated short-term, quick-fix solutions to productivity problems so as to maximize the "bottom line." For example, as Stauffer (1982) points out, U.S. business and industry can no longer afford to practice short-term-gain management by cutting costs without regard for long-term technological superiority. How this is accomplished will vary from situation to situation (e.g., placing engineering expertise at higher managerial levels). However, it will require top-level management to change their ethics (values)-in-use and the social structure of the work environment they create to a long-term commitment to technological research and development.

A shift to a long-term view of organizational profitability, productivity, and survival dictates relatively permanent solutions to productivity problems so as to maximize the long-term well-being and survival of the organization. In fact, it is just such an operational ethic (value)-in-use that is being touted by some (Ouchi, 1981; Pascale and Athos, 1981) as being at the very heart of Japanese corporate industrial success. In reviewing the cluster of work factors that have been identified as being culture-specific to the Japanese management orientation (Ray and Eison, 1983), four major factors are evident: group agreement, futuristic approach, product quality, and commitment (see Table 2). Again, it is not as important that these factors can be identified as it is that collectively the four factors provide an overall code of behavior—a stated ethics (values). The essence of that code is that long-term product quality is achieved by consensus commitment. Commitment may well be the crucial factor—participants agree to make decisions together in an atmosphere of com-

Table 2

Comparison of Several Work Factors
in Japan and Western Counterparts*

WORK FACTORS	FACTORS DEFINED	JAPANESE	WESTERN COUNTERPARTS
1. Group Agreement	Membership seeks to arrive at agreements	Accepted systems to compromise for achieving common purposes, participatory management	Unionized interaction system or adversary within system, competition and limited trust within
2. Futuristic Approach	Long-term commitment to corporate improvement	Fast payoff and short-term benefits are not all as banking system demands long-term savings program: management is permanent, promoted from within	Sales program geared to short-term profits and personnel promoted on basis of quick success—not long-term planning; management transitory, high rate of mobility among employees
3. Product Quality	Explicit concern for high quality control on products	Individual pride and competition to produce quality items with low reject rates	Sales effort emphasizes numbers at the expense of quality
4. Commitment	Whole is greater than sum of parts	Individual makes life-long commitment to organization and country	Individual's right to "do own thing" emphasized; self-enhancement takes precedence over group welfare

*Adopted from Ray, C.M. and Eison, C.L. *Supervision*. Chicago: The Dryden Press, 1983.

mitment. Such an ethical value appears to be in direct conflict with the "merger mentality" evidenced by the leadership of many American corporations. Based on their study of forty-two successful American companies which had survived twenty years or more, Peters and Waterman (1982) concluded that the major function of top management was to orchestrate the organization's value system. It appears that this cannot be done by defining the system-wide stated ethics (values) but by facilitating the match between the stated-ethics (values) and the ethics (values)-in-use.

The Solution

Simply put, the solution to productivity problems in the United States lies in the cultural values practiced by the management of our business organizations. That is, the solution to the productivity problem in the United States today lies in realizing there is a discrepancy between the stated ethics (values) and the ethics (values)-in-use of management. It is our contention that effective management is possible only when consistency exists between the stated ethics (values) and the ethics (values)-in-use of management AND when those ethics are consistent with the major values held by the organizational work force.

Signs of such a management orientation are already evident among American business (Deal and Kennedy, 1982). Long-term, people-oriented values are not only being reflected in marketing slogans but also in figures and objects being used to symbolize organizations. And, almost all of the time, the major selling point is that the value preached is the value practiced by the management of the organization—that there is a consistency between management's stated ethics (values) and the ethics (values)-in-use. For example, General Electric's "Progress is our most important product" is not only espoused by the organization's management but is practiced by them also.

The increase and maintenance of high levels of productivity in our society is possible: our citizens generally possess values consistent with a productive work ethic (Eison and Craig, 1982). However, the low productivity levels generally observed for the American worker are in part a function of the inconsistency between management's stated ethics (values) (that are, for the most part, consistent with employee values) and the ethics (values)-in-use of management (which generally are not consistent with employee values). Therefore, management strategies implemented to increase employee productivity will fail to register any long-term gains UNLESS they are integrated into the values of the individuals who comprise the social structure of the work place. There must be greater consistency between management's stated ethics (values) and their ethics (values)-in-use.

REFERENCES

Cummings, T.G. and E.S. Molloy. *Improving Productivity and the Quality of Work Life*. New York: Praeger Publishers, 1977.

Deal, T.D. and A.A. Kennedy. *Corporate Cultures*. Reading, Mass.: Addison-Wesley, 1982.

Eison, C.L. and J.R. Craig. *Productivity and Reciprocity: Know your BVD's!* Unpublished manuscript, 1982. (Available from C.L. Eison Department of Psychology, Western Kentucky University, Bowling Green, KY 42101.)

Kaplan, A. *The Conduct of Inquiry*. San Francisco: Chandler, 1964.

Ouchi, W.G. *Theory Z: How American Business Can Meet the Japanese Challenge*. New York: Avon, 1981.

Pascale, R.T. and A.G. Athos. *The Art of Japanese Management*. New York: Warner Books, Inc., 1981.

Peters, T.J. and R.H. Waterman, Jr. *In Search of Excellence*. New York: Harper & Row, 1982.

Ray, C.M. and C.L. Eison. *Supervision*, Chicago: Dryden Press, 1983.

Stauffer, T.M. "Management Orthodoxy Challenged." *Educational Record*, Summer 1982, pp. 56-57.

Stone, M. "Ethics: Making a Comeback?" *U.S. News and World Report*, December 8, 1980, pp. ?

Fair Approach
to Work Attendance

Jeffrey C. Claypool

In past decades, business magazines, newspapers, and professional journals have published numerous articles deploring the high absenteeism rate in American business. These articles have described ways of controlling, reducing, computerizing, and even solving the absentee problem. After reviewing much of the data available, it appears the problem has not been solved or the overall magnitude of the problem reduced.

Recent estimates tag the national absence bill somewhere between $15 and $20 billion a year (Drucker, 1974). This appears to be a conservative figure, but it still represents a considerable loss of productivity and a waste of human resources.

The Bureau of Labor Statistics defines absenteeism as follows (Jucius, 1971):

Absenteeism is the failure of workers to report on the job when they are scheduled to work. It is a broad term which is applied to time lost because of sickness or accident that prevents a worker from being on the job, as well as unauthorized time away from the job for other reasons. Workers who quit without notice are also counted as absentees until they are officially removed from the payroll.

The Bureau of Labor Statistics has conducted an analysis of national data on absence from work that quantifies the amount of time lost. The results are listed below for review:

In May 1976, more than 3.6 million nonfarm wage and salary workers, who usually work full time, were absent all or part of the reference week because of illness, injury, personal, and civic reasons. Of every 100 workers, 6.4 had an absence.

Time lost through absence totaled about 82 million hours per week, or 3.5 percent of the usual hours of all nonfarm wage and salary employees who regularly work full time. The loss represented about one and a half hours per week for all employees.

Lost time per absent worker averaged 22.7 hours, representing about 56 percent of their usual work-week.

If rates of absence in May 1976 were representative of the full year, the average worker would have an absence in 3 out of 52 weeks. Over the year, total time lost because of illness, injury, personal, and civic reasons would average about 9.1 days per worker.

Illness and injury accounted for more than three-fifths of all absences and about two-thirds of the total time lost in May 1976.

About one-third of all absent workers were out at least a week, losing, on average, about 41.5 hours per week. The majority of absences lasted less than 1 week, averaging about 13 hours, or fewer than 2 days. Although the incidence rate was greater for part-week absences, more than 60 percent of the total time lost in May 1976 was attributed to absences of a week or more (Hedges, 1977).

Absences resulting from vacations, industrial disputes, or weather conditions are excluded from this study (Hedges, 1977).

The implications of the previously mentioned statistics are serious. Poor attendance has contributed to large operating losses and, for some companies, pulled their competitive position below the survival level. Many observers have implied that *absenteeism is one of the major factors pushing the United States in the direction of becoming a second-class economic power.*

The absentee problem is not confined only to the United States. Referring to Canada, Brian Kendall states that

There's a disease afflicting business and industry in this country so costly that the revenue lost to strikes is trivial by comparison. It's called unnecessary absenteeism, and it costs Canadian industry about 130 million work days every year—more than thirty times the number of days lost to strikes. "Unnecessary absenteeism is costing Canadian industry more than $8 billion a year," says Bob Holliday, President of Industrial Health Assistance Ltd. in Toronto. That figure includes costs for training surplus workers to fill in for absentees, for expensive benefit packages, for disruptions in production, and for perpetual overstaffing (Kendall, 1979).

Why should this long-standing and costly problem continue at its existing level despite the research, experience, and knowledge that is possessed by the industrial world today? There are many reasons that might be offered, several of which are below:

We give up and get frustrated trying to solve a problem that shows no improvement and exists on a continuing basis.

We conveniently adopt the idea that people simply do not care.

We still do not know enough about the research and psychology of the attendance problem.

We have not made full utilization of the knowledge available due to lack of supervisory training regarding the attendance problem.

We spend more time disciplining employees about the problem than counseling to correct the deficiency.

We fail to establish an attendance program with specific and well-defined guidelines. As a result, most employees and supervisors do not understand what the rules are. Moreover, this does not allow the supervisor or the employee to know what action will result from a future absence and they become afraid to discuss the trouble causing their absence from work.

It is this last point of not understanding what the rules are that we should observe more closely. W. Edwards Deming, a consultant who is best known for his work in Japan, which commenced in 1950 to create a revolution in quality and economic production, recently stated that most people on a job (and even in management positions) do not understand what the job is nor what is right or wrong. Moreover, it is not clear to them how to find out. Many of them are afraid to ask questions or to report trouble (Deming, 1982).

It would appear that Mr. Deming's comments about the job also apply to attendance when we view a vague and unclear statement found in many attendance policies, such as the following: "Excessive or unwarranted absences will lead to disciplinary action up to and including discharge." Is it possible to understand the meaning of this statement? More important, can supervisors and employees understand it? Can they state what actual number of absences are unacceptable and do they know what disciplinary action will be taken if further absences occur?

In far too many cases, supervisors and employees do not know the answers to these questions. Many programs make the answers vague intentionally. This avoids a commitment to a course of action. Many managers and supervisors believe that this allows flexibility and makes their jobs easier. It also delays talking to employees about the unpopular topic of specific disciplinary action and possible discharge. It is easier to talk to employees in terms of generalities, but it is not the best approach. People have a need to know where they stand. Why not establish a program with specific guidelines that will allow employees to control their own destiny, allow them to know where they stand at any given time, and know what specific corrective action will be taken if further absences occur?

Consider the following question: "If your continued employment and financial security depended on one particular performance area, would you prefer specific or vague instructions?" Most will respond that specific instructions are preferred. Why would employees respond differently?

The Development of a Reasonable Attendance Program

It is from this standpoint that we begin the next segment of this paper. The program that we are about to discuss was developed and implemented at one of our manufacturing facilities. We recognized we would not eliminate totally our attendance problem. So, instead, we chose to reduce our average monthly absentee rate by establishing well-defined, fair, and consistent guidelines. Prior to the implementation of this program, the average monthly absentee rate at this facility had steadily increased over a five-year period from 3.6% to 5.5% per month. Now, two and one-half years after the introduction of the program, our average monthly absentee rate has been reduced to 4.4%. Even more important than the decrease in the absentee rate, we have accomplished a major objective of equal treatment regardless of what department or area an employee works in. Many facilities have never developed a specific plant-wide attendance policy and, therefore, there is no uniformity from department to department in determining attendance performance. As observed earlier, general guidelines without specific terms or conditions will not be understood by a majority of employees.

Our attendance policy has been divided into several areas and was reviewed with all employees in small group meetings prior to implementation. The policy which is listed in the employee handbook, is below.

Attendance

You were hired to do an important job and it is important to be at work on time every day.

When you are absent or tardy you have a loss of wages and a mark on your attendance record. Your fellow employees lose because they may absorb extra duties which a replacement may not be able to perform efficiently. Your Company loses, too. Quality, safety, and productivity all suffer when you are absent. Please read and become familiar with our written attendance guidelines, which are as follows:

Absence and Lateness Policy

An absence will be recorded as either a Class I or Class II absence.

Any reason for absence not listed under Class II absence will be considered a Class I absence.

Class I Absence (Most Controllable)
Employee sickness or non-factory injury, without doctor statement;
Personal business;
Absent—no report;
Car trouble;
Weather.

Class II Absence (Least Controllable)
Jury duty;
Military duty;

Death in immediate family (per policy)—mother, father, sister, brother, son, daughter, wife or husband of the employee;

Funeral of—mother-in-law, father-in-law, sister-in-law, brother-in-law, grandparent, grandchild, stepmother, stepfather, stepsister, stepbrother, stepson, or stepdaughter of the employee or spouse;

Factory injury;

Hospital confinements;

Employee sickness or non-factory injury, documented with doctor's statement submitted to your supervisor within two weeks of your return to work;

Family sickness of a—mother, father, sister, brother, son, daughter, wife or husband documented with doctor's statement submitted to your supervisor within two weeks of your return to work;

Authorized factory, department, or job shutdown;

Leave of absence—sick;

Leave of absence—personal.

Unreported Absence

Any absence not reported to your supervisor is a Class I absence.

An employee having three (3) consecutive unreported absences will be terminated.

Lateness

Each lateness or early quit during a calendar month will count ½ point as a Class I Absence. Lateness or early quits due to the items outlined under a Class II absence will not be counted.

Probationary Employee

Once the ninety-day period is completed, the attendance record will reflect the number of days missed from the ninety-first day of employment.

Leave of Absence

Days off due to an approved leave of absence granted by the Personnel Department will not be counted as a Class I absence. No personal leaves of absence will commence until this approval by the Personnel Department has been obtained.

Written Warnings

Written warnings will be given for excessive absences, early quits, or lateness according to the schedule listed below. This is done to provide ample notice to the employee that his/her record indicates a serious attendance problem.

No. of Class I Absences (cumulative)	Corrective Action
5	Written memo
8	Written memo
11	Final warning
12	Termination

Perfect Attendance

Means no absence in a calendar month other than jury duty, scheduled vacation, military duty (total of four weeks annually excluding weekend reserve duty), death in the immediate family (up to three days by policy), and authorized factory, department, or job shutdown. Employees missing work because of a layoff, factory injury, hospital confinement, sickness lateness, early quit, leave of absence, or other reasons not listed will not be considered to have perfect attendance.

Rewards to Improve Your Attendance Record

An employee may improve an absence record through improved attendance. One absence will be deducted from the employee's record as a reward for each calendar month worth of perfect attendance. Once an employee has zero points on his/her attendance record he/she will receive one credit point for each month of perfect attendance up to a maximum of three (3). Employees missing work because of a layoff, factory injury, hospital confinement, sickness, lateness, early quit, leave of absence, or other reasons not listed will not have the reward described above deducted from their attendance record, or will not receive any credit points.

Total Absences

After earned rewards have been credited, any employee having twelve Class I absences in a twelve-month period will be terminated on the twelfth absence.

Centralized Call-In Procedure

If there are times when you must be absent or tardy, your supervisor should be notified at least one hour prior to your shift. These are methods of reporting your absence and tardiness:

1. The preferred method is for you to contact your immediate supervisor.
2. If you are unable to reach your supervisor you must call and leave a message which will be mechanically recorded. When reporting an absence you must state your name, supervisor, department, reason absent, and the expected duration of absence.

Remember, the best method to report an absence is to call your immediate supervisor.

Many reviewed the program with skepticism. Comments were made that a specific guideline program such as this would irritate a majority of employees. To the contrary, many employees applauded the program and stated their appreciation that a positive program had been put forth to control a problem that affects their job, their compensation and their job security. The program has been in effect at the facility since October 1, 1979 and only one modification has had to be made. Several employees suggested we establish a credit point once their absence total reached zero. This would allow an employee who had reached zero points and then had a month of perfect attendance to have a -1 accumulated total. The next month, if the employee missed one day, he or she would then have zero points again. The maximum credit points that could be established was limited to thirteen points.

We attempted to make the program specific and detailed. Standards have been established and it has been imperative that we adhere to each of them. The program also has allowed us to achieve a greater amount of consistency with respect to attendance and lateness. Each employee has been treated equally, utilizing the same guidelines. Supervisors in all departments now have the same standards with respect to attendance. Our corrective action program has consisted of oral discussions, written memos, and final warnings prior to the termination of employment. The written warning schedule listed on a previous page has taken the place of the progressive disciplinary program that usually consists of oral warnings, reprimands, suspensions, and discharges. It is hard to justify economically giving an employee with an attendance problem additional time off because of a disciplinary suspension. This defeats the objective of getting the employee to work on a regular basis and adds additional costs to a problem that is already too expensive for business and industry.

An important procedure in our absentee control program has been to keep accurate records of absences and lateness. The records have been kept on a daily, weekly, and monthly basis. Records have been necessary to compute the absentee rate and they have been utilized to determine what items are contributing to the problem. Accurate records have specified which departments and supervisors are experiencing the most serious problems. Responsibility for maintaining attendance records has been assigned to the employee's supervisor. The Personnel Department advises and serves the supervisor with requested audits, counseling, and corrective action.

A computer program was developed that lists the date of absence or lateness of each employee, number of work hours lost, reason for each absence, day of the week, department, supervisor's name, class code, shift, and whether a doctor's statement was submitted. An updated listing is issued to each department on a weekly basis.

The problem of absenteeism is a very complex one. In many cases, it may appear to be unsolvable. This attitude is just as undesirable as the absentee problem itself. Perhaps this attendance program, or some of the concepts outlined in it, will be applicable to your facility or business. Or you may have found that the recommendations have only served as thought provokers. The important thing is to establish a program with specific and well-defined guidelines that can be understood easily by all employees and supervisors.

REFERENCES

Deming, W. Edwards. "Improvement of Quality and Productivity through Acting by Management." *National Productivity Review*, 1982, p. 20.

Drucker, Peter F. *Management: Tasks, Responsibilities, Practices.* New York: Harper & Row, 1974.

Hedges, Janice N. "Absence from Work—Measuring the Hours Lost." *Monthly Labor Review*, October 1977, pp. 16-30.

Jucius, Michael J. *Personnel Management.* New York: Richard D. Irwin, 1971.

Kendall, Brian. "Combating Absenteeism." *Atlas World Press Review*, September 1979, p. 51.

Participative Management...
Professional Suicide or
Organizational Murder?

Donald W. Cole

Professional suicide is often not "suicide" at all, but rather a kind of organizational "murder" in which the brightest and most committed employees get killed off in a professional sense by the very organizations that are most badly in need of the talents they offer.

The term "professional suicide" was coined by a major aerospace corporation to describe a phenomenon they had observed on their own staff. After a period of three to five years with the company, some of the brightest, most talented, and hardest working employees would either begin to deteriorate or leave the organization. Some would:

1) Quit their jobs for other jobs far beneath their capabilities.
2) Become disruptive and do things for which they must have known they would be fired.

3) Quit working and gradually retire on the job.
4) Fail to keep up with the technology and allow themselves to gradually become outmoded.
5) Develop physical complaints of a classically psychosomatic nature such as backaches, headaches, ulcers, etc.
6) Let themselves deteriorate to a point where they appeared headed for gradual physical suicide through excessive weight gain or the pressure of their schedule.

The organization took the onus of blame off itself by calling the process "suicide." A clinically trained counselor was hired to help these employees with what the company had decided was their problem.

This tendency toward blaming the victim is fairly typical. Most organizations spend a considerable amount of money recruiting high achievers. After they are hired, however, most of these people are left pretty much on their own. Management recognizes that machinery needs overhaul but is only gradually coming to appreciate that employee knowledge and skills must also be maintained.

When employees are recruited they are often made promises about the rewards for hard work. If they give their all, they are told, then someday they might be president or at least general manager.

After a while, though, some of these workers find that they are working harder and harder and their careers are going nowhere. Gradually, disillusionment sets in.

Suicidal Tendencies

The personality structure of those who get caught up in "professional suicide" can gradually be described as "entrepreneurial." These are people with strong achievement needs and a strong desire for accomplishment. They are primarily concerned with the means by which results are achieved.

In contrast to the typical bureaucrat, who has well-developed survival skills and is expert at sensing who is prone to "professional suicide," they have little interest in the development of survival skills. Instead, they become single-mindedly committed to an objective and often alienate their bosses and the organization in their drive to achieve this goal.

People who end up committing "professional suicide" or being "killed off" have usually reached a point in their careers where they are no longer motivated by any of the common fears. They are not influenced by the fear of survival, the fear of social disapproval, the fear of God, or even of the Big Boss. They are confident in their ability to survive, whether it be in this organization, some other organization, or on their own.

Such people do not want to be told how to do their job. Professionally secure, they believe that it is their responsibility to get a certain job done and they don't welcome any direction on when, where, or how to do it.

Standard operating procedures are often jettisoned as they seek better and quicker ways to reach their objectives. This creates problems for bureaucratic organizations that want not only a standard end product but also a standard way of getting it.

The fact that these people are creative and hard workers does not protect them indefinitely. Traditional managers, who are used to expecting conformity, usually find ways to squeeze them out, fire them, or bury them.

The result can be viewed as "suicide," since these people do court their own fate by refusing to conform to the traditional organization and the traditional management style. Or it can be looked at as a kind of organizational "murder," because the organization has not yet learned the management skills necessary to sustain this kind of worker.

Management by Assumptions

Assumptions about people are crucial to the whole management process. The assumption that managers have about people are, in the end, the determinant of how an organization will be managed.

Most organizations have had a good deal of experience in sending managers away to management training courses. At these courses, the managers are told how to manage better. And yet, when they get back to the organization, very little changes. Why? Because people manage on their assumptions about people, not on rules of management. And few management development courses address these assumptions.

The problem is not so much that managers hold false assumptions but that their assumptions are incomplete for dealing with today's organization.

Over and over again, I hear managers and supervisors yearning for the "good old days." They long to go back to the past, when the management technology that they know worked. Not having kept up, they find themselves unable to adapt to the next attitudes that call for new management techniques.

The problem is not, as many of these people claim, that workers no longer respond to management. The problem is that today's workers have to be approached differently and managers don't know how.

Just as there have been generations of computers, each capable of performing more than the last, there have also been generations of management theory, and later managerial models have incorporated sophistications that earlier styles did not have.

In his book, *Scientific Management*, published in 1911, Frederick Winslow Taylor taught that man is primarily motivated by economic incentives and will do that which promises the greatest economic gain. He also taught that the people were not capable of a high degree of self-discipline and self-control and, therefore, had to be controlled by external forces in order to insure their working toward organization goals.

In spite of what we have seen happen to the "rate-buster," the person who works with the single goal of increasing his or her paycheck, many organizations are still being managed by the assumption that this person is typical.

There has been a lot of learning about people and how they work since 1911. And a lot of this knowledge is not being put to use.

Geometric Progress

When I draw a triangle for a group of managers and tell them that it represents Pyramidal Management with the boss at the top, managers and supervisors in the middle, and workers at the bottom, their faces light up with recognition. Everyone knows this managerial style. It is the method in which most managers have been trained and the pyramid is the managerial model that most managers carry around in their heads.

When I draw an upside down triangle and tell a group that it stands for Inverted Pyramidal Management, only a few faces show any sign of recognition.

As organizations become more complex, the top executives begin to realize that they don't and can't know everything and so they begin to rely more heavily on the people who are in contact with problems to correct them. Instead of the communication flowing from the point of the triangle (the boss) to the base (the workers) as it does in Pyramidal Management, the base is now called upon to inform the point. In order for this system to work, the boss must be supportive of the supervisors and the supervisors of the workers.

After the system has been explained, many managers begin to recognize that they have experienced this type of management, although they haven't discussed it or given it a name.

There is an essential weakness to the Inverted Pyramid, which becomes apparent when you look closely at the structure. The whole organization rests on the point, creating an unstable situation and putting tremendous burdens on the executive level. Eventually this pressure builds up to create a bottleneck and, as the organization grows and technology becomes more complex, the problems of this style become more intense.

The most obvious solution is to broaden the point, which gives us a square. In a typical group of managers, some may have heard of Matrix Management but few have yet experienced it.

In Matrix Management there are a series of bosses—functional bosses, concerned with the various organizational functions, and project bosses, concerned with the numerous projects going on throughout the organization.

The major practical difficulty with Matrix Management is that it violates the basic rule of Pyramidal Management which says that each person will have only one boss. Instead, each person has two bosses, a functional boss and a line boss.

Dealing with two bosses instead of one requires a whole new set of skills. If these new rules of the game are not clearly explained, as is often the case with translation taking place gradually over a number of years, this setup can create a great deal of stress for employees. This stress is left untreated in many cases because the organization does not recognize the fact that new skills are required.

Eventually the situation will become even more complicated. More and more high-technology companies have had to adopt a management structure known as Circular Management. In Circular Management, each person has many more than two bosses and these may change from time to time with little or no notice.

The Circular Management model developed out of the aerospace industry. Since no one person could be expert in the wide variety of skills and technical information necessary to launch a space capsule, leadership had to rotate, depending upon who was expert on the subject of the moment.

Because of the complex way in which materials influenced decisions on propulsion and these decisions, in turn, affected considerations of life support, which influenced package size and so on, teamwork was essential. Managers found themselves working as often for peers as for the person whose name appeared above theirs on the pyramidal line chart.

Although Circular Management is in many ways more satisfying and more effective, implementation can be problematic. People have to learn a whole new set of skills—interpersonal competence skills, how to get things done when you don't have the power to fire people, synergistic decision making, how to make teams out of committees, how to get team decisions instead of committee decisions, how to confront sensitive issues and problems, how to feel comfortable discussing their own feelings and emotions as well as the feelings and emotions of others. None of these are skills that are recognized or encouraged in the average organization.

Most organizations recognize the need for change and do attempt to plan. But, despite these efforts, the same old problems emerge. Plans do not materialize because of differing management philosophies. Worthwhile programs are buried in committee, because there are not enough staff members willing to buck the system. Professional employees exhaust creative energy in conflict and competition with one another. Distrust takes root and informal cliques and power groups inhibit mutual productivity. A sense of insecurity and futility infects staff people. Gradually, things grind to a halt.

But it doesn't have to end this way. Change, which is so essential for survival in today's climate, can be brought about smoothly and effectively. Managers, subordinates, line and staff, technical and professional and clerical employees can work together productively. It is possible to develop a total atmosphere which generates innovation and creativity, increases job satisfaction, develops positive interpersonal relationships and fosters participation in defining and reaching individual and organization goals.

Planning for Prevention

Professional suicide is preventable. Organizations can avoid the problem by:

1) Employing Organization Development professionals to review the human system and how people are working together. At least some of these people should be external to the organization. Sole reliance on internal resources tends to create a situation, which may be called corporate "in-breeding," in which the organization produces an image of change while, in fact, perpetuating traditional values, policies, procedures, and problems.

2) Creating a Management Development program to improve the cooperative working skills of its managers. Many bright professionals get killed in the cross-fire between two managers.

3) Making real use of a performance evaluation system so that your employees have a chance to find out where they stand. Open job posting also indicates a commitment to openness in the organization while allowing employees to seek their opportunity inside the organization.

Managers can make a great difference in the statistics on professional suicide. The best antidote is a manager who:

1) Is not threatened by the knowledge and skills of subordinates.

2) Is able to communicate about what is wanted or not wanted.

3) Is open enough to coach subordinates on organizational pitfalls and opportunities.

Women in Positions of Leadership: Problems They Face

Kathryn L. Herkelmann

As more and more women ready themselves for managerial positions they must be prepared to fight not only socialization, but also traditional stereotypes, prejudices, and the role expectations of others in order to survive. Women who want careers as managers must learn to deal successfully with problematic differences in assumptions, perception, and behavior because they are women. The residues of past socialization cannot be changed but must be accepted, and the woman must move forward from that point. Hennig and Jardim (1976) suggest that women must identify these aforementioned residues and learn to manage them. The most critical step in this process is the decision whether one really wants to succeed in a management career. This choice to be a manager will require competition primarily with men in a system that men understand better and with which they are more familiar. In this process of preparing for leadership roles, women must not only receive support but also give it

166

to others. The participative management style of leadership could be used by women when addressing the support issue. Putting to work the philosophy of participative management also may help them to avoid a common occurrence identified by Hart (1980) who states that women who have "made it to the top" often forget those behind them. The involvement of employees in problem solving, decision making, etc., will keep leaders in contact with employees at all levels.

Women and Leadership Roles

Kantor (1977) suggests some familiar cliches concerning a woman's lack of potential for organizational leadership roles: "No one wants to work for a woman" and "Women are too rigid and controlling to make good bosses anyway." There is evidence showing a general cultural attitude that men make better leaders. This preference for men is a preference for power. The problem with women as leaders is, first, that there are often doubts about how far they can go in a corporation and, second, that there is a widespread belief that women can only be individual "movers"—if they can move they will not be able to take anyone else with them. Many studies have found that neither men nor women want to work for a woman. However, it should be noted that women are more willing than their male counterparts to work for a female supervisor. Not only do individuals not wish to work for a woman supervisor because of some long-held stereotypes that a woman boss is petty, controlling, and a busybody; but working for a woman carries less status than working for a man.

The current emphasis on team building rather than the high-handed traits and techniques of the traditional industrial supervisor puts the leadership role in a new arena. *Women may be better equipped than men to adjust to the new requirements of effective leadership.* The prototype of the tough, authoritative leader is no longer advocated or effective. The traits that women have been criticized for in the past appear to be the attributes of the future. A woman is accustomed to the role of a catalyst, incorporating the ideas and contributions of others to encourage teamwork. She is used to and able to tolerate more informality and to function in a less authoritarian manner (Josefowita, 1980).

What Can Women Do to Become More Effective Leaders?

There are several steps a woman must go through if she wants a career in a management position. First, the woman must accept that the residues of difference between men and women will always be with us. For example, the woman may always be more vulnerable to criticism that is directly personal than a man; or she may find it difficult to be aggressive and to initiate activities in her own cause. These residues need to be identified and managed. Secondly, she must make the decision that she really wants to succeed in a management career where there is much competition and in a system with which she is not familiar. A woman must be able to say with confidence that she wants a career and that she is willing to confront the problems she will inevitably encounter. She must be far more specific in her planning than the men around her and even more alert at anticipating situations that accentuate pressure in areas of particular vulnerability. She must be able to manage her environment and herself concurrently (Hennig and Jardim, 1976).

Women must also begin to develop relationships with people in the organization over and beyond those they see in the day-to-day course of their work. Key individuals must be identified who will be important in making promotion into and success in the next job possible. Women need sources of support, advice, and information beyond that of the traditional system, a support group made up of other women. They must set limits on competing among themselves for unrealistic reasons. An informal system can help women identify leadership opportunities in other areas of the company. It can also help to identify male managers who are particularly supportive of women.

Because most corporations reward employees for doing a good job ("hands on" work), people find it difficult to delegate when assigned managerial responsibilities. "An effective manager must change from a doer into a motivator (Hart, 1980). Because of the tasks women are traditionally assigned, this change to becoming a motivator may be a difficult transition. The use of a participative leadership style may help make this transition a successful one. It will force the manager to take the time to interact with employees by soliciting ideas or giving feedback. Asking for input will help take the task completion out of the leader's "hands."

Hennig and Jardim identify the critical concepts of *trust, sharing,* and *the ability to depend on.* When a person assumes the role of leader the job becomes that of a coordinator of people, and this cannot be done solely by relying on one's self. It requires the ability to trust in, depend on, and delegate to others, especially one's peers and subordinates. As manager, one must behave in ways that foster credibility. It means being able to motivate subordinates by creating a climate that is open enough for employees to work and grow within the environment.

As the woman assumes a leadership role, the successful supervisor keeps uppermost in her mind that she is a supervisor, not a *woman* supervisor. She must learn to differentiate between her professional and personal self; she must also learn to keep her emotions out of the job. All decisions are to be made based on the facts. Women also must learn that one of the first rules in this game of business is to prepare a successor for your own job. One cannot move ahead until there is someone to take her place. Often this is a reality that few women understand. Leaders advise women supervisors that the more sincere an interest they demonstrate in each individual, the harder the employees will try and the more willing they will be to share ideas and work with the supervisor.

REFERENCES

Hart, Lois Borland. *Moving Up—Women and Leadership* (New York: AMACOM, 1980).

Hennig, Margaret and Anne Jardim. *The Managerial Women* (New York: Doubleday & Company, Inc., 1976)

Josefowita, Natasha. *Paths to Power—A Women's Guide from First Job to Top Executive* (Reading, Mass.: Addison-Wesley Publishing Co., 1980).

Kantor, Rosabeth Moss. *Men and Women of the Corporation* (New York: Basic Books, Inc., 1977).

Acknowledgments

"Ethical Behavior and Mental Health in Organizations" by Joseph Cangemi was published in *KACRO Journal* (*Journal of the Kentucky Association of Collegiate Registrars and Admissions Officers*) as "Ethical Behavior and Mental Health", Vol. 11, 1983.

"A Pragmatist's View of Participative Management" by Joseph Cangemi was originally an invited address presented to the American Institute of Industrial Engineers, 1982 Gainsharing Conference, Washington, D.C. and reproduced in *Gainsharing, A Collection of Papers* under the title of "Participative Management As a Foundation of Quality of Work Life—Some Observations." It was published in the August, 1984 issue of *Organization Development Journal* under the same title as appears in this book.

Donald Cole's award-winning article "Professional Suicide or Organizational Murder?" was published in *Northeast Training News*, November 1979, pp. 9 and 19.

The article by Casimir J. Kowalski and J. Richard Bryson, "Participatory Management in Organizations of Higher Education: Leadership Mandate for the 80's," was originally published in *Psychology— A Quarterly Journal of Human Behavior*, Vol. 19, Number 2/3, 1982, pp. 22-27.

"Participation as a Method of Conflict Resolution" by Josip Obradovic was originally published in *Conflict Resolution Technology*, published by the Organization Development Institute, Cleveland, Ohio, 1983.

"The Scanlon Plan and Employee Participation" by William Taylor and Joseph Cangemi was published in *Psychology—A Quarterly Journal of Human Behavior,* Vol. 20, I, 1983, pp. 43–46, as "Participative Management and the Scanlon Plan."

The authors would like to thank the editors of the above noted periodicals and publications for permission to reprint the articles indicated.

Index

173